THE MOST FUN YOU'LL HAVE AT A CAGE FIGHT

THE MOST FUN YOU'LL HAVE AT A CAGE FIGHT

a memoir/MMA *primer*
RORY DOUGLAS

HELL PRESS
UNIVERSITY OF HELL PRESS

This book published by University of Hell Press.
www.universityofhellpress.com

© 2015 Rory Douglas

Book Layout and Cover Design by Olivia Croom
http://bit.ly/oliviacroom

All rights reserved. No part of this book may be reproduced or transmitted in any form or by any means, electronic or mechanical, including photocopying, recording or by any information storage and retrieval system, without written permission from the publisher, except for the inclusion of brief quotations in a review.

Published in the United States of America.
ISBN 978-1-938753-17-6

for MBW

CONTENTS

Chapter 1
My Brother Fights Another Man in a Cage 1

Chapter 2
A Reductive History of Mixed Martial Arts 13

Chapter 3
Everything that Goes on Before a Title Fight 27

Chapter 4
Chad's First Title Fight 39

Chapter 5
Amateur MMA Gone Even Wilder 49

Chapter 6
Wrestling and MMA 59

Chapter 7
About as Far Behind the Scenes at an MMA Event
as You Could Possibly Want to Go 67

Chapter 8
Introducing Billy Walker 79

Chapter 9
The Return of Chad 91

Chapter 10
A Fight That No One Really Wanted to See . . . 103

Chapter 11
Losing a Belt in the Most
Humiliating Way Possible. 109

Chapter 12
Billy's First Title Fight 123

Chapter 13
Introducing Jonny Gilbertson. 135

Chapter 14
What Happened to Flat Top 145

Chapter 15
Chad's Last Amateur Fight 149

Epilogue 159
Acknowledgments 175
About the Author. 177

CHAPTER 1

MY BROTHER FIGHTS ANOTHER MAN IN A CAGE

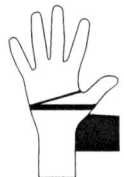

TONIGHT I'M GOING TO Edmonds Community College in Lynwood, Washington to watch my oldest brother, Chad, age 25 and a well-paid scientist with the Boeing Company, fight another man inside a cage. The fight will end when either Chad or his opponent is unconscious or taps out, or when the three rounds end and the judges decide who delivered the worst beating.

No one's making Chad do this. He's not even getting paid. He's been fighting guys in cages for a year or so, training two hours a day after work and fighting every few months. He's been fairly successful so far, winning three fights and losing only once. There's a chance that if Chad's successful enough and keeps at it long enough he'll advance to the low-level pro ranks, where he could get paid in the high three figures for showing up to a fight and even more for winning.

Chad's fight is one of 15 fights this evening, all part of an event called *Ax Fighting 24: Domination*. No axes are involved. No one who organizes the fights has a good explanation for the name. It seems that "Ax" is being used as an intensifier, like "cool" or "awesome." Let's hope it catches on.

The name of the actual sport being practiced tonight is *mixed martial arts* or MMA, as it's usually known. This is a sport that combines the most effective parts of all types of hand-to-hand combat—jiu-jitsu, Muay Thai, wrestling, boxing, and so on—which means that it's basically what you'd imagine: an all-out, few-holds-barred fight, in a cage.

AT THE GYMNASIUM

The line is out the door. I'm standing there with our youngest brother, Jake, a fifth grader at a local Christian academy. We're in the line for people who, like us, wisely bought their $25 tickets ahead of time, a line that is somehow not moving. In front of me an adult male is wearing a T-shirt that reads, "I LIVE ON THE CORNER OF BITE BE BLVD AND NO FREAKIN' WAY." I'm trying to imagine a universe that makes this T-shirt a plausible wardrobe option—maybe he actually lives at the intersection of streets with these names—but I'm rescued by Jake, who's using his 11-year-old powers to cut in line, and I'm not about to lose him in this crowd.

In addition to Jake, I'm here tonight with the rest of my immediate family: my brother Brady, 20, his girlfriend Emily, and my mom and dad who are trying to straddle the line between not really encouraging the whole mixed-martial-arts cage-fighting thing and supporting their oldest son. I have a pen and a notebook and I intend on using both, because I am the sort of person who carries a small leather-bound notebook in his pocket and writes in it during amateur sporting events.

The attendees are mostly white. Caucasian, yes, but more pasty, Washingtonians-in-January white. In the crowd of roughly 2,000, I count seven people of color. In sight range there are eight heads shaved to the skull. I'd estimate the crowd is 80 percent male. No matter how many spotlights and posters and amps you put in a community college gym it still looks like a community college gym: basketball hoops folded to the ceiling, plaques celebrating sad athletic accomplishments, wooden bleachers designed with a total disregard for the human sitting position. And it's crowded. We had to get here an hour early just to grab seats for our cluster of friends and family. Somehow, despite the January temperature outside, inside the gymnasium it's about 85 degrees and humid.

Before the fights proper, the lights dim and six people dressed in either black karate outfits or their dads' bathrobes enter the ring. They each have a different type of weapon: nunchaku, sword-like objects, sticks. Music begins playing—fast-tempo angry dance music. One by one these people—can't be older than 20, any of them—step to the center of the ring and perform a choreographed routine of what looks like karate combined with interpretive dance. The crowd is silent. This little performance art act seems out of place as an opening bit for cage fights. You can feel the word "pussies" hovering unspoken in the air. Someone behind me whispers, "Girls only want boyfriends who have great skills." The routine ends and the crowd erupts in applause.

Before every fight, when each fighter walks out to the ring from a back door with his posse—usually his coach and training partners and gym mates—someone plays a song over the gym's sound system. I don't know what the songs are supposed to express—the fighter's taste in music or worldview or just something to get him jazzed before the fight—but they're usually angry rap or angry rock or an angry combination of the two. Jake states that his song would be "Our Song" by Taylor Swift.

It would be great if I could record the name of each song and then compare that fighter's performance to his or her song. I have a hypothesis that the angrier the song the worse the fighter, or at least the fighter's performance. It seems that the last thing a fighter needs before fighting is a jolt of anger, since athletic performance usually depends more on clearheaded judgment than on wild anger and since most of the fighters appear to have anger to spare regardless of their soundtrack.

I'm unable to note the songs because I'm distracted by someone I'll call Franklin. He looks like Franklin the Turtle from the Canadian educational cartoon. He's standing on the gym floor just below our seats. He's wearing thick glasses and is chubby. He appears to be unaccompanied. As soon as each intro song begins playing, he immediately begins dancing, head bobbing, and generally just rocking out, even if the song doesn't lend itself to rocking out. While dancing, Franklin looks around the gym, using the head bobs as a sprinkler-style way of moving his gaze. His expression is that of a young man looking for ladies. Except for those in my immediate family, Franklin is my favorite person in the gymnasium.

Because this is one of the first MMA events I've attended, I don't know enough about what's going on to give an accurate play-by-play of all the fights. So instead I spend the time until Chad's fight assembling a list of moves the fighters use and what I think they might be called.

AN INCOMPLETE LIST OF FIGHTING MOVES
AS I'VE NAMED THEM TONIGHT

1. **The Go Fuck Your Mother, I'm Too Angry to Throw a Sophisticated Punch**

   The GFYM punch is most often seen from a fighter in his first fight. It's basically an uncontrolled punch motivated more by the desire to throw a really, *really* hard punch that may or may not connect than to use any sort of fighting strategy, e.g., the holding of gloves in front of the face, the dodging of punches. It's almost endearing in its simplicity. I suspect the GFYM punch is the result of listening to Insane Clown Posse or misogynist rap music before the fight.

2. **The I'd Fuck My Mother, But I'd Have to Go to the Cemetery and Dig Her Up Punch**

   The IFMM punch is thrown in response or simultaneously to the GFYM punch. Equally angry, it often misses its mark. It seems like its owner is thinking, *Nuh-uh, no one throws a wildly ineffective punch at me and gets away without receiving an equally wild and ineffective punch.* I imagine that whoever runs these fights deliberately pairs up the GFYMers with the IFMMers. Neither of them would last long with a more strategic opponent.

3. **The FYI, Your Elbow Doesn't Bend That Way**

   I would need a protractor, a compass, and two well-made mannequins to properly diagram this one. Basically Guy One takes Guy Two's arm and leverages it so that his elbow starts bending in the opposite direction from how an elbow joint traditionally bends. When done properly, this results in Guy Two tapping out, the mixed martial arts equivalent of crying uncle. I've heard that some fighters are so determined to never tap out that they will simply let the fight end when their elbow shatters. Fortunately, (I think) this doesn't happen tonight.

4. **The I Will Rip Your Fucking Head Off**
   During the first fight, a GFYM/IFMM bout, someone behind me encourages his favored fighter to, "Rip his fucking head off!" *A bit excessive*, I thought. But then, lo, in the next fight, in the first round, when they're standing up, Guy One somehow shoves Guy Two's head down so that he can python-wrap it with his right arm, and from there he simply lifts the body by the neck/head area, squeezing it in a way that makes me think of how the little yellow heads pop off of LEGO pirates.

5. **The Spinning Roundhouse Kick to the Face**
   Turns out it's actually quite effective.

6. **The Raining Hammers of Thor**
   My personal favorite, the RHOT is simple: one guy sits on the other guy's chest, punching the guy on bottom in the face again and again and again. Usually a fight-ender.

7. **The Let's Hold Each Other's Heads While We Knee Each Other's Bodies**
   Self-explanatory. Let me note that prior to tonight, I always considered knees the Segways of attack

moves, neat but largely useless. I now know I'd rather be punched in the jaw than kneed in the ribs.

8. **The Climbing the Cage, Straddling the Padded Top Bar, and Riding It as Though It Is a Horse or Perhaps a Woman**
This one happens after the most entertaining bout of the evening, between two athletic African American males. The come-from-behind winner of this match, a man who quite accurately calls himself Flat Top, performs this move after his victory.

INSIDER'S VIEW OF
OUR FELLOW AUDIENCE MEMBERS

Observation confirms that it'd be tough to find a natural female hair color in the room tonight. Brady comments that this place is full of the sort of girls who could do a number of simple things to improve their looks—go for a jog in the park, eat better, buy a flattering turtleneck—but instead get breast enhancements.

The epitome of this approach to beauty or attractiveness or sexiness or whatever it is they're going for is the ring girls. These are the girls who do a lap around the cage between rounds holding up a sign noting (for example) "Round 2." These girls wear nothing but heels and a tiny swimsuit. At least one of the girls went to my high school and wasn't a renowned beauty even by the generous standards of 17-year-old boys. They're not bad-looking girls, but now, with the spotlight on them, booty shaking around the ring with all these mostly male eyes on them, they're in the unenviable spot of being not-bad-looking girls trying really hard to be model-caliber, Photoshopped beautiful girls.

And I don't think it's just me who thinks this. In the row in front of me is a group of guys who seem like they'd be in an Edmonds Community College frat if Edmonds Community College had frats. When one particular ring girl, who looks like she's a perfectly healthy weight for her height, comes out to announce a new round, one of these guys quips, "She'd look a lot better on my bed." No one really laughs or nudges one another and even the guy seems like he said it out of obligation, because this is the sort of thing people like him are supposed to say about girls in bikinis under spotlights, and not because he felt any real attraction for her. And I think the Edmonds Community College frat guys and I and everyone else at *Ax Fighting 24: Domination* would agree: the opposite of sexiness isn't ugliness. It's sadness, confusion, and pity.

A HEAVYWEIGHT FIGHT

In the red corner we have a guy who has a record of one win and no losses. His name sounds vaguely familiar—turns out he wrestled heavyweight for a rival high school around the same time I was a high school wrestler. His opponent in the blue corner weighed in at 300 pounds and has a record of no wins and four losses. Because of his size and his hair color I assume that everyone who knows him calls him Big Red.

Big Red's record brings up the question of how many beatings a person has to take before he's not allowed to fight anymore. One would assume that after a few losses most people would decide the whole fighting thing isn't for them, or else the fighter's coach would step in and have an uncomfortable heart-to-heart with the loser—*what else could you call him?*—about this maybe not being his particular cup of athletic tea. Or, if all else fails, you'd think other fighters would just stop agreeing to fight the loser, since there's nothing to gain from beating someone who has never won a fight, and if you somehow lost to the loser you'd be the only guy the loser ever beat.

Franklin is still dancing to the intro songs. He pauses for a moment to text message. I can tell from the expression on Franklin's face that the recipient of this text message is someone with whom Franklin is interested in having sex.

The fight begins, and within nine seconds Big Red has been thrown into the cage. For a moment he's squished there, his fat squeezing through the squares in the fencing. Big Red is then thrown to the ground and punched in the face five or six times, and the fight is over. No one really cheers. The whole thing is just too depressing. One of the Edmonds Community College Frat guys in front of me says, "Let's go drink beer and fuck people."

CHAD'S FIGHT: 155-POUND MMA

Chad comes out with his posse, his coaches or buddies or whoever, people I don't know, definitely not his Boeing friends. His song is by a band called Flogging Molly. Franklin is rocking. The fighters tap gloves at the beginning of the fight. I'm not sure how tough Chad's opponent is supposed to be. Someone near me states that Chad is trying to avoid getting punched. After a few seconds Chad takes his opponent down by grabbing both his legs and charging until the guy falls on his back. Someone in our little cluster has distributed fruit snacks but neglected to give me any.

The other guy is on his back with Chad on top. Apparently you can do plenty of terrible things to your opponent while on your back. Most of these things involve depriving your opponent of oxygen or bending him in undesirable ways. Chad's opponent has his legs wrapped around Chad. Neither fighter can do much from here. They're grappling for position with slight hip shifts and a game of who-has-whose wrists. If someone gains decisive control the crowd will stand up, since most of these people are educated enough MMA fans to detect the subtle difference between a stalemate and an imminent shit beating. No one is currently being punched or bent. The gym hasn't cooled off at all. The sweat on my arms might be other people's sweat that has evaporated and condensed onto me.

A large part of the audience stands up. Chad somehow tucks his opponent's arms under his (Chad's) legs, leaving my brother perched on his chest with nothing between Chad's fists and his opponent's face. Thor's hammers begin to rain. My brother is in a cage in front of hundreds, maybe thousands, of people punching another man in the skull again and again and again. The ref blows a whistle. The fight is over. Chad wins by technical knockout in the first round.

WHY

When people find out that my brother is a mixed martial arts fighter, they tend to ask, "Why? Why would someone volunteer to fight another person? In a cage? Why would anyone spend their Saturday evening giving or receiving a not-very-many-holds-barred beating?"

It's an interesting question, and I never have a great answer to give. Since I'm more or less fraternally obligated to attend amateur MMA events for the duration of Chad's career, I plan on pursuing this question, figuring out why exactly Chad or anyone else would take up amateur mixed martial arts.

But at the same time it seems it might be more interesting to withhold judgment of MMA and its people as much as possible—sometimes it's just not possible—and observe, enjoy, and keep this question in the back of your mind, *What the hell is going on here?*

CHAPTER 2

A REDUCTIVE HISTORY OF MIXED MARTIAL ARTS

IF YOU WANT TO learn how exactly MMA came about, my view is that it's best to look at it within the larger context of mankind's attempts to answer one of humanity's oldest questions, *Who's the best fighter? Quien es mas macho? Who's the person who could beat up any other person on earth?* If we put two guys in a field or a ring or a cage or some similar contraption and don't let them use any weapons—the who's-best-with-what-weapon query is a whole different but also very important field of study—then, *Who's the guy who would absolutely dismantle any other guy?*

The Ancient Greeks were one of the first cultures to tackle this question. The Greeks laid the foundations of Western philosophy, invented forms of government still used today, and discovered some neat things about triangles, so of course they tried to figure out who the best fighter in the (Greek) world was. Their way of doing this was a sport called "pankration," a combination of boxing and wrestling that allowed all moves except eye gouging and nut shots. Pankration was the toughest Greek martial art, and thus the best pankration fighter in the Greek world could claim to be the toughest guy in the known world with pretty much scientific certainty.

Pankration's real claim to fame is an incident that might be the greatest moment in the history of martial arts, mixed or otherwise. During a pankration match, Guy One got Guy Two in a chokehold and, as Guy Two was passing out, Guy Two broke Guy One's toe causing Guy One to tap out. Guy Two won the match, but he had gone so long without oxygen that, by the end of the fight, he was dead. Yet he still won the match, even though his opponent killed him. (Dying isn't the same as tapping out.) For a brief moment, the best fighter in the Greek world was a dead man. This was also one of the last times where anyone could truly say who the toughest person in the world was.

Pankration wasn't the only Greek martial art—they also had wrestling, a type of boxing, and various hand-to-hand combat techniques used for military and personal purposes—and, obviously, the Greeks weren't the only society to have martial arts. According to Chinese legend, the Chinese Yellow Emperor had already given the world Kung Fu way back in the fifth century B.C. JuJutsu, an ancestor of Judo and jiu-jitsu, began in Japan in the 1500s, and JuJutsu itself was a combination of several earlier Japanese martial arts. Muay Thai, Thailand's big martial art, really came into its own in the 19th century. Boxing got its modern start in England in the 17th century and got way more awesome when America took it over. It seems that part of having an advanced culture is having your own special way to beat people up.

It's all more complicated than this—these are only a few of the world's martial arts, and each of these martial arts has its own history and variations—but the upshot is that by, say, the first part of the 20th century, humanity had all these diverse and highly developed and neat ways of beating people up, but what we'd gained in mixed martial arts technique we'd lost in knowledge. No one knew which of these options was the best way to actually beat someone up. We understood Planck's constant and could build flying machines, but we didn't know whether a good wrestler could beat up a boxer, or how a Muay Thai guy would fare against a jiu-jitsuan, or whether karate would be any use at all against a tough guy at a bar, or what about tai chi? We could discuss it and write think pieces and make SWOT charts—

WRESTLING
Strengths: Grappling; mat work; probably the slipperiest fighters.
Weaknesses: Wrestlers have likely never been punched in their life; cauliflower ear; ringworm; mat herpes (real thing—look it up).
Opportunities: Just shoot in on the other guy's legs real quick and hope nothing bad happens.
Threats: Getting hit/kneed/slapped/stomped, etc.

BOXING
Strengths: Can punch real hard; can get punched real hard. Just look at those guys.
Weaknesses: Kicking.
Opportunities: Punching real hard.
Threats: Pretty much any move that doesn't involve a fist.

JIU-JITSU
Strengths: Probably throws or spin kicks something.
Weaknesses: Don't know. I don't think they allow elbows in jiu-jitsu.
Opportunities: I imagine fighting someone who knows jiu-jitsu is sort of like when you played *Street Fighter* against someone who knew all the special moves.
Threats: I'm sure all of this info is available online.

TAI CHI
Strengths: Okay, so we're not seriously going to discuss tai chi as a martial art. Instead, in the space allotted by this SWOT Analysis, I'm going to tell my one and only tai chi anecdote.
Weaknesses: I once worked at a coffee shop where at least once a week—I kept track—a customer would order a tai chi. This was not a drink on the menu. It was not a secret drink. We sold other drinks. We sold lattes, mochas, and chai teas. But we did not sell tai chi.
Opportunities: So I came up with this big plan that the next time someone ordered a tai chi I would do an elaborate slow-motion karate chop—I had seen old men doing this in the park—and then say, "Okay, now what would you like to drink?"
Threats: Needless to say this would have been funny to absolutely no one but myself, and also needless to say I wasn't a good fit for the coffee chain in question, and we parted ways before I had a chance to give someone their tai chi.

—but we didn't really have a way to determine how each martial art stacked up against the others.

By around the middle of the 20th century, at the very latest, we had the means—air travel, electronic communication—to figure out who the toughest guy on earth was, yet we didn't do it. We had the World Cup to determine the best soccer team on earth, the Olympics to determine who could swim the 50-yard butterfly the fastest, the Olympics to determine who could swim the 100-yard butterfly the fastest, and an annual dictionary-length book of pointless world records that someone took the time to document and verify, yet we didn't arrange an event to figure out who could beat up whom. Maybe we didn't truly want to know who the best fighter in the world was. Maybe we knew that this was ultimately a metaphysical question that we could never empirically answer. Maybe we knew that if the toughest person in the world knew he was the toughest person in the world he'd be a total dick about it. Maybe. But the most practical reason that we didn't immediately settle the who's-the-toughest-guy question is that we had boxing.

Boxing was by far the most popular martial art in the Western world in the second half of the 20th century. The heavyweight boxing champion was known as the toughest fighter on earth, not because he earned that title by defeating the top guys from all the other fighting disciplines, but because everyone said so, including the boxers themselves. Boxing had enough cachet and revenue that it had nothing to gain by having its best square off with someone from another martial arts discipline. It's what high school wrestlers deal with when they wrestle a girl: if you beat a girl, congrats, you beat a girl, hope you feel like a man. But if you lose to a girl, you lost to a girl. Likewise, if a boxer beat a wrestler or jiu-jitsuan or whatever, he just confirmed everyone's assumptions. But if he lost, boxing as a whole risked giving some of its legitimacy and revenue to another sport.

But what if boxing aficionados could figure out a way to cash in on mankind's pressing desire to know who the toughest guy is without risking any of boxing's legitimacy or revenue-generating abilities? Well, in 1976, the reigning heavyweight-boxing champ was Muhammad Ali. He was toward the end of his best boxing years, but he was at the height of his shit-talking powers. One day, for unknown reasons, Muhammad started mouthing off about how no one from Asia could beat him in a fight, so Antonio Inoki, a professional Japanese wrestler, volunteered to fight Ali using a combination of wrestling and boxing.

This seemed like it could be a good first step in determining the actual toughest fighter on earth. We'd get to see how one of the best boxers of all time matched up against a great wrestler, and then we'd have some evidence on which sport was the more effective fighting technique, and maybe it would spur further interdisciplinary matchups. However, pretty much everyone with any knowledge of the fight reported that the thing was completely and thoroughly fixed and was simply arranged as a moneymaking monster for all involved. Then reports came out that maybe the whole thing wasn't fixed after all and was actually a real fight. The fight had the potential to be an all-time classic: America versus Japan, boxing versus wrestling, it's-not-fake versus yeah-it's-totally-fake. The fight itself was a boring 15-round draw that was obviously fake and ended with the crowd throwing trash into the ring and demanding a refund.

So. The boxing world wouldn't be much help in developing a somewhat rigorous way to determine who the best fighter on earth was. They already had their answer, and most people accepted it.

Around this same time (the 1970s and '80s), in Brazil, there was a feud between two clans who practiced similar but philosophically different styles of jiu-jitsu called Vale

Tudo and Luta Livre. Anyone not well-versed in the nuances of jiu-jitsu would have a tough time distinguishing the two styles, so it seems that the feud had more to do with bad blood and family loyalty than with trying to prove which fighting style was more effective. For decades the Vale Tudo clan fought the Luta Livre clan in bloody battles, both sides honing their fighting styles and talking crap. And it turns out that when you and your clan dedicate your entire lives to defeating another clan through a particular version of jiu-jitsu, you get pretty good at that particular version of jiu-jitsu.

It was never definitively decided whether Vale Tudo (Portuguese for "anything goes") was better than Luta Livre ("free fighting"). The feud finally came to some sort of an end in 1997 at a show in Rio pitting the two styles against each other, where, before the event could even properly get underway, fights started breaking out in the crowd. The event soon turned into a full-on riot, which the actual fighters joined. One of them even got stabbed. That was the last of the feud, at least in public.

But at that point, Vale Tudo—and its main practitioners, the Gracie clan—had already won the marketing war. In the late '80s one of the Gracies, Rorion, came to Southern California and started telling people that he could beat anyone in a fight. And he did. Wrestlers, boxers, tough guys—he beat all takers. It turned out that all the submissions and chokeholds from the Gracie style of Brazilian Jiu-Jitsu were almost impossible to stop if you weren't really good at Brazilian Jiu-Jitsu.

It seems that Rorion's quest was initially motivated less by money and more by pride in Vale Tudo and pride in being a Gracie. But if you have a guy who has thus far beat up everyone he's tried to beat up, there's money to be made there. Rorion had set up a gym to teach his fighting style and two of his students were advertising executive types who pitched him an idea: they would hold a contest where any type of fighter could battle any other type of fighter without any rules. Rorion was on board, but added that if they were going to do this, it should be in a cage to keep the fighters from falling out of the ring. It was decided that there would be no time limit, no rounds. At one point someone suggested that the cage be surrounded by a moat filled with alligators, but history doesn't record why that idea didn't stick. This became a contest, the first Ultimate Fighting Championship (UFC) event, held in Colorado in 1993.

To represent the Gracie family, Rorion chose one of his younger brothers, Royce. Rorion considered Royce the wussiest Gracie, and thus it'd be all the more impressive if he won the UFC tournament. And win he did. Royce, at 180 pounds, beat up on some much larger competitors, including a guy by the name of Ken Shamrock, who, as though that name didn't sound fake enough, sometimes worked under the nom de plume *The Toughest Man on Earth*. Royce and Rorion and the Gracies could now make a credible claim that the Gracie style of Brazilian Jiu-Jitsu was the most effective ass-kicking method since the dawn of time.

This event was the start of MMA proper, although it wasn't actually called mixed martial arts until 1995. This first event was profitable enough and promising enough that it spurred further UFC events. Royce won three of the first four such events, and the only reason he didn't win UFC 3 was that he didn't really feel like fighting anymore after winning a particularly long bout. It was soon clear that if someone wanted to beat Royce, not only would he have to learn Gracie Jiu-Jitsu, but he'd also have to do something to improve upon it, and he'd have to bring in techniques from other disciplines, and then adjust them to work in the new sport of MMA. Thus, the true mixing of martial arts began.

It's sometimes tough to separate the history of MMA the martial art from the history of the UFC, the biggest MMA league, especially in the early days of the sport. But there's an important difference: if MMA was created to answer one of mankind's ancient questions—*Who's the best fighter on earth?*—then the UFC was created to answer an even more ancient question, *How can I make a crap-ton of money?*

It's interesting that the promoters used the word "Ultimate" in their product's name. In the early- to mid-'90s "Ultimate" was typically used in much the same way as the "Ax" in *Ax Fighting*—as an intensifier meaning "the best" or "coolest" or "raddest." But the people who named the UFC must have been at least slightly aware of the word's traditional denotative meaning: last, decisive, conclusive, the final say, the end of the line. The UFC and mixed martial arts in general do seem like the end of some sort of line, a sport taken as far as it can go in a certain direction—or at least that's the way it's marketed.

It's probably fair to say that the ultimate aspect of the sport is what caused the UFC so many problems in its first years. Throughout the '90s and early 2000s, the Ultimate Fighting Championship battled state athletic commissions and broadcasting corporations to even stay on pay-per-view. A few powerful people—most notably Senator John McCain, who called MMA "human cockfighting" and who, it should be noted, was on the record as a huge boxing fan—weren't keen on televising something that billed itself as no-holds-barred fighting. It didn't help that in the early days the

UFC didn't use basic safety measures like weight classes or having fighters fight only once per night, although the rules did quickly evolve to make the sport slightly less brutal and immensely more marketable.

In 2000, a college dropout and former boxing promoter named Dana White, along with his friends Frank and Lorenzo Fertitta—executives at a major casino and thus quite wealthy—paid $2 million for the UFC. Because of all the problems getting sanctioned as well as televised, the UFC at that point was a money-losing venture. White and the Fertittas were basically paying for the UFC name. But it just so happened that the Fertitta brothers—who, as mentioned, were executives at a major Nevada-based casino—somehow had strong connections with the Nevada State Athletic Commission, and soon the UFC was sanctioned to operate in Nevada, which meant that they could hold UFC events in the state and distribute them outside the state via pay-per-view.

The UFC continued to lose money into the mid-2000s, but when you're a massively wealthy casino magnate you can fund pet projects out of your personal pocket. Dana White and the Fertittas adjusted the UFC rules and marketing, but what really got the UFC on solid financial ground was an undeniably smart idea: White and the Fertittas convinced Spike TV to air *The Ultimate Fighter*, a reality show the UFC folks had dreamt up about MMA fighters competing for a spot in the UFC. "Convinced" isn't quite the right word. "Paid" is probably better. The UFC—i.e., the Fertittas and their deep casino-fed pockets—paid all the production costs for the show, more or less the equivalent of giving Spike TV $10 million.

The Ultimate Fighter was a hit, as far as a reality show about people kicking the crap out of each other could be a hit, and the season finale put up a respectable 1.9 on the

Nielsen ratings and couldn't have scripted a better fight than the one between Forrest Griffin and Stephan Bonnar. Along with the subtle interpersonal conflict of the best reality shows, *The Ultimate Fighter* had the overt physical conflict of guys literally fighting for a spot in the UFC. What wasn't there to like? Probably the most brilliant part was that Dana White arranged for two of the most famous MMA fighters at that time, light heavyweights Chuck Liddell and Randy Couture, to coach the rival teams on *The Ultimate Fighter*, and after the end of the first season the UFC held the long-awaited Liddell versus Couture title fight—and they held it not on Spike TV but on pay-per-view. The pay-per-view fight attracted 300,000 viewers, double the best previous UFC event. Because of *The Ultimate Fighter*, Dana White and the Fertittas got even more filthy rich, and the UFC became a massively popular, almost-mainstream sport that your typical young adult American male was well aware of.

The UFC succeeded in figuring out a way to make an immense amount of money. It's estimated that the UFC is now worth more than $1 billion. But then there's still the question we started with: *Who's the best fighter on earth?* MMA has answered this question better than any sport since the days of pankration. In the early days of MMA, it was established that a good jiu-jitsuan would beat a good fighter from any of the other martial arts. And then, when Ken Shamrock won UFC 6—the Gracies had dropped out of the whole operation at that point, but their fighting style lived on—he showed that someone proficient at the new sport of MMA would beat a pure jiu-jitsuan. So, you could make a case that we now have an answer to one of the oldest of questions: the heavyweight champion of the highest MMA league—the UFC—is the best fighter on earth.

It's an answer, but it's imperfect. If you want to quibble with one of man's most impressive additions to our body of collective scientific knowledge, there are at least four quibbles you can use:

1. **The UFC isn't a scientific nonprofit dedicated to the unbiased study of the toughest fighters on earth.** The UFC is a ruthless business and knows that you make more money off of fighters who draw crowds than off of excellent but uninteresting fighters without a fan base. So, the UFC is much more interested in finding the most popular and marketable fighters than in empirically determining who the best fighters are.

2. **Technically, the heavyweight boxing champion of the world never lost his toughest-man-on-earth title, so, can a UFC champion truly claim to be the toughest man on earth if he never previously defeated the toughest man on earth?**

3. **Performance-enhancing drugs. Are you still the toughest man on earth if you used performance-enhancing drugs to become the toughest man on earth?**

4. **For all we know the true toughest man on earth is chopping logs with a dull ax somewhere in Siberia and doesn't give a fuck about the UFC.**

So, while we now know that MMA is the most effective martial art we have—a piece of knowledge that in itself is a huge addition to the world's body of scientific research—it's probably fair to say that we still don't truly have an answer to the question of who the toughest man on earth is, and we likely never will.

But, for the subject at hand—amateur mixed martial arts in the Seattle suburbs—we don't need an answer. For the average guy, the question of who's the toughest person on earth is an abstract Zen koan compared to the much more compelling question of how tough you are. Who cares about being the toughest guy on earth, what if you could be the toughest at your school? What if you walked into a bar and everyone knew you were the toughest guy there? Because of *The Ultimate Fighter* and the UFC's popularity, lots of mostly young and mostly male Americans knew about MMA, and they now knew that it was the best way to get tougher, and knew that they could now take up MMA for themselves and figure out how tough they were—and show other people how tough they were—if they were the kind of person interested in that type of thing.

Chad qualifies as that kind of person. When Chad was in middle school, his Instant Messenger screen name was "CDExtreme34." As far as screen names go, it was a prescient description of one aspect of Chad's personality: doing things to the extreme. To wit, he owned and wore a leather jacket in high school. He wrestled from seventh grade on, and would blast Limp Bizkit on the way to school at 7:00AM to get pumped for a match that evening. He attended flight school at Embry Riddle in Daytona Beach, getting his commercial pilot's license and a degree in aeronautical engineering in three years, while maintaining a near-perfect GPA. After college, in his first years at Boeing, Chad had a successful extracurricular career as a semi-professional wakeboarder and even competed in an event on the wakeboarding pro tour. One time, Chad drank so many energy drinks that he couldn't drive and had to go to the hospital. Extreme. So it was only natural that Chad would take up mixed martial arts, the most effective, the most extreme martial art, a sport where he could gauge just exactly how tough he was.

CHAPTER 3

EVERYTHING THAT GOES ON BEFORE A TITLE FIGHT

IN JUST UNDER TWO weeks, Chad will fight Jonathan Moore for the *Ax Fighting* 145-pound title, which according to Chad is more or less the amateur mixed martial arts championship for the greater north-Seattle area. It's been more than seven months since Chad's fight at Edmonds Community College, and in the meantime he's won three more fights. None of these fights were huge deals in their own right, but they built Chad's record to seven wins and one loss, good enough to earn a shot to fight for a title belt. But it gets better. That one loss came in Chad's first fight at the hands of, yes, Jonathan Moore, the same Jonathan Moore Chad will now fight to try to avenge his loss and win a novelty-size belt and a waist-high trophy. The whole thing is similar to the plot of *The Mighty Ducks 2*.

Before a fight, Chad trains after work four times a week for two to three hours. Chad does this training at Charlie's

Combat Club, located in downtown Everett, not far from Puget Sound. Everett is my hometown—and Chad's, and our whole family's—and is best known for being the place that smells terrible when you drive through on Interstate 5. The smell is from the paper mill.

From the outside, the building that houses Charlie's Combat Club looks more like a hardware store than a place where people learn to beat the crap out of each other. Within a few blocks of Charlie's there are several payday-loan stores, and you wouldn't have to go much farther to find an adult-novelty store. Whenever I drive through Everett near Charlie's, there are always just plain weird-looking people walking or sitting on the sidewalk. This is not necessarily connected with Charlie's Combat Club but is interesting nonetheless.

Charlie's Combat Club is owned and operated by Charlie himself. Any male who's physically large and not a total asshole is often described as "just a big teddy bear," but Charlie actually resembles a medium-sized teddy bear—thick chest, short arms, not that tall—a teddy bear who not only knows a few dozen ways to choke and break and generally harm you, but can teach other teddy bears to do the same. Charlie is also genuinely nice, a quality I've been told teddy bears also possess.

Charlie was a fighter himself, back in the days before the UFC when all-out fights were held in bars and barns and back alleys. Charlie has retired from fighting—he's 40—and runs the gym as a full-time job. Along with organizing *Ax Fighting* events and mentoring his trainees and doing the administrative work to keep the gym running, Charlie also works out with his elite-level fighters four days a week. Whatever money Charlie makes from the gym and *Ax Fighting*—and I've heard it's quite a bit—he works for it.

Over the next 12 days, Chad, like most athletes before a major competition, will taper off his training. No more heavy sparring or running up mountains, as a group from Charlie's Combat Club did last weekend. For this fight, Chad isn't tapering off as much as he normally would, since his training was set back by a rough case of cauliflower ear. If your ear gets batted around long enough, it'll start to look like cauliflower, and it'll feel tender and fragile like an over-boiled vegetable, way too tender to receive a punch during practice.

Chad now has a pus-draining valve installed in his ear, and he's wearing protective headgear that I'm pretty sure he stole from our middle school's wrestling team. His cauliflower-related staph infection has subsided, so he's trying to get in a few more days of aggressive training before he starts tapering for the title fight. Notebook in hand, I'm accompanying Chad to Charlie's Combat Club to see how exactly someone prepares himself to fight for the most prestigious 145-pound amateur mixed martial arts title in the north Seattle suburbs.

AT CHARLIE'S COMBAT CLUB

A sign on the gym door reads, "Please leave your ego at the door. If not, someone might take it from you." I'm walking in with a diary-sized notebook and a chewed up pen so that I can scribble things in said notebook—things, it'll turn out, like "snow smurf" and "6 push-ups + 3 push-ups = 11 push-ups"—so any ego I started with was obviously left in the car with my library copy of *Swann's Way*.

In the gym's small reception office, I pick up a membership price sheet titled *Charlies Combat Club*. It crosses my mind to ask Charlie if there's more than one Charlie involved with the combat club or if he just forgot an apostrophe, but I can't imagine an enjoyable conversation that starts like this. And I'd bet that no one around here dwells on things like standard apostrophe usage, apostrophes neither bringing in more paying gym customers nor helping you kick the shit out of people.

The training area of the gym is about half the size of a basketball court. About half of it has blue gymnastics mats fixed to the floor and walls, and the other half has free weights, punching bags, and electronic cardio machines that make the same beeping noises that all electronic cardio machines make. Sally, one of the female fighters who trains at Charlie's—and who is ranked fifth in the world for 125-pound women's MMA—is on an elliptical machine.

Above the cardio machines is a loft reached by a narrow stairway. A square cage takes up the entire loft, except for a small coaching strip on the side. The cage is about a fighter and a half tall—almost all the amateur fighters I know are between 5 feet 7 inches and 5 feet 11 inches—and about 15 feet per side. The pricing sheet I'm carrying states that the cage is available for rentals.

Charlie and Billy, one of Chad's training partners, are on the mats, and someone is filming them with a camcorder. Charlie is on his back, describing what he's doing. I gather that they're filming a tutorial for something that Charlie calls side-control escape. The gist of side-control escape, as I understand it from this brief tutorial, is that when you're on your back, if the person on top can arrange things so that his body is perpendicular to your body—his hips not on your hips—you're in trouble. But if you, the person on bottom, can do a side-control escape so that your opponent's body is parallel to your own body—chest-to-chest, hips-to-hips—you're not so immediately screwed and your defensive and even offensive options increase.

When the camera guys stops filming, Charlie explains that this move is also known as "the cheerleader." He follows this explanation with a pantomime demonstrating why the move is called the cheerleader, which I don't understand but assume is indecent.

In the corner of the mat, about eight feet from the bench I'm sitting on, a child, probably around ten years old, is lazily wrestling with a dummy. The dummy is blue, about 36 inches long, and is constructed of three spheres, decreasing in size, like a snowman. On the side of the dummy in marker is written "75 pounds."

The child is chubby and has a dreadlock-style ponytail that, mid-neck, splits into two ponytails, as though it got caught midway through mitosis. I'm unable to determine whether the child is a boy or a girl. He/she appears to be unaccompanied. Maybe someone is using Charlie's Combat Club as childcare.

At a normal practice like this, the elite fighters like Chad aren't learning new moves, or even intentionally drilling moves. Instead, they warm up and then they spar, perhaps with some weight training or cardio mixed in. The emphasis is on sparring, though, since sparring involves cardio and, more importantly, is the best way to refine technique. As Rorion Gracie proved in the early days of MMA, technique is vastly more important than general badassery. If your average tough guy (or girl) throws his or her hat into the MMA cage against someone who may not be as ripped or tattooed but who knows his MMA stuff, the tough guy will likely end up bent into an undesirable shape.

For a real-life example, let's say that you fancy yourself an above-average athlete who wrestled in high school and did pretty well at it—let's say, I don't know, you placed sixth in the Washington State 4A high school wrestling tournament at 145 pounds in 2003, your senior year—and then let's say you decide to roll around with your 87-pound 11-year-old brother (let's call him Jake Douglas) who has gone to a few kiddie-type MMA classes. And then you soon find yourself unable to breathe because Jake has octopussed himself around your neck and you, unable to pry him off, start losing your peripheral vision, so you have to resort to repeatedly standing up and then dropping your much younger brother onto the floor much harder than is probably ethically acceptable until he's finally jarred loose.

Back to the gym. Chad and Eddie—one of the coaches at Charlie's—and Billy and Charlie are wrestling on the mats. The wrestling is all subtle shifts of their arms and hips, jockeying for position without ever doing anything with that position. Watching people warm up is boring. It now makes sense why sports movies often use a quick montage to represent months of training. This is slightly more exciting than watching other people jog.

The pricing sheet in my hand says prices range from $40 a month for the bronze level—which means you can use Charlie's facilities but don't receive any training—to $125 for the gold level, which includes classes and fighter training. All levels require a one-year commitment. You can be billed each month or pay for the entire year up-front, with a small price break for up-front payment. Except for the silver level. The silver level is $99 a month or $1200 for a year up-front. You can do the math on this one, and then you can be the one to tell Charlie how he might better structure his pricing system.

Chad tells me that quite a few people sign up for several months or even a year of training and a gym membership, thinking that they'll get into MMA or at least get into MMA shape. I'm told that only 15 percent of these people actually end up sticking with the gym for any length of time. I suspect that this 15 percent number is made up on the fly and is not being pulled from a spreadsheet in Charlie's office. To cancel their membership, these people have to talk to Charlie and essentially tell him that they're too much of a wimp to continue training at his gym—or, worse, they'll try to come up with an excuse to cover up the fact that they're a wimp. I'm told that quite a few of these people just opt to continue paying the monthly fee rather than have this conversation with Charlie.

The blue snowman dummy is now on top of Ponytail. Ponytail is struggling, trying to escape from under the dummy, which is lying perpendicular across Ponytail's chest. Maybe I should intervene. This might be a training exercise. After a few minutes of struggle—it might be feigned struggle, though—Ponytail escapes from under the dummy, using what I believe is the aforementioned "Cheerleader."

The sheet in my hand says that Komodo Kids Submission Wrestling starts in about five minutes. Maybe Ponytail is warming up before class starts. He—I'm now pretty sure it's a boy, though I can't state exactly why—stands for a moment, then lifts the dummy to a standing position. No one else is watching. Ponytail, holding the dummy by the head, knees it in the middle snowball. He lets it fall to the ground. He glares at the snowman before he sits on the bench to rest.

Chad and Eddie and Billy and Charlie are now wrestling with more intensity. Sweat has turned Chad's shirt from light gray to dark gray. Charlie is cleaning some Billy blood from his shirt. They take a water break, and then Billy and Chad walk up to the cage to spar.

A large man has appeared in the gym and is talking to Ponytail. This man has dreadlocks that look like they could have given birth to Ponytail's smaller dreadlock. Ponytail walks over and says something to Eddie that I don't hear, to which Eddie kindly responds, "I'll tell you when I think you're ready." Evidently, Ponytail was asking when he could have a real MMA fight.

Now that the gym is quieter I notice that a radio has been playing in the background. As Billy and Chad enter the cage by way of a training montage song, "The Climb" by Miley Cyrus comes on the radio. They start sparring, and almost immediately someone gets slammed into the fence, and Charlie is yelling some coaching tip at them, some way to better slam each other into fences.

THE DAYS BEFORE THE FIGHT

Most serious fighters don't fight at whatever weight they happen to weigh. Instead they fight at a much lower weight than what they walk around at—roughly 12 percent of their bodyweight lower, though that number can vary quite a bit from fighter to fighter. Chad, for example, weighs a lean 165 pounds when he's not preparing for a fight, but fights in the 145-pound weight class.

Chad loses that 20 pounds by a process fighters and wrestlers and boxers call "weight cutting." Weight cutting is a totally different animal from dieting. In the weeks before weigh-ins, a fighter slims down as much as possible. This part is similar to traditional dieting: less food, fewer calories, lots of exercise. A lean fighter will probably lose about four percent of his bodyweight this way.

The unintuitive part of weight cutting—and the truly difficult part, as far as self-control and discipline go—comes in the 48 hours before weigh-ins. At this point what matters isn't the calories or nutritional value of a food or drink but its actual weight. The timeframe is too short for long-term metabolic processes to matter. You're not going to lose 12 pounds of fat or muscle in two days. So, since most of the weight in our digestive systems comes from water, short-term weight cutting is all about dehydration.

In the day or two before weigh-ins, fighters usually abstain from liquids and do their best to sweat incredible amounts. Eating is almost a moot point. If you've ever been severely dehydrated and severely hungry at the same time, you'll know that all but the most liquid-based foods seem repulsive. Something virtually weightless like potato chips would be permissible—except for the salt, of course, which hinders your sweat output, according to weight-cutting tradition—but would be entirely disgusting when you're that dehydrated.

Weight cutting isn't exactly an approved medical science, so its nuances are more based on lore and hearsay than any real scientific evidence. It's said that if you're jogging, you'll sweat more if you stop to do push-ups or sit-ups every few minutes. Saunas will make you sweat but will exhaust you in a way that exercise doesn't. Sucking on ice cubes helps make the dehydration more bearable. Popsicles are more enjoyable than ice cubes but don't last as long. Laxatives might be tempting but are prone to make you sick and mess up your stomach. Your hair doesn't weigh enough to merit shaving it for weight purposes.

The weigh-in setup for amateur MMA actually encourages severe weight cutting. In most high school wrestling competitions, weigh-ins happen only a few hours before competition, which means that wrestlers don't have sufficient time to undergo massive rehydration efforts. High school wrestlers still cut weight, of course, but the short gap between weigh-ins and competition directly hampers the practice since severe dehydration doesn't exactly help your athletic performance. Compare that with amateur mixed martial arts, where weigh-ins happen 24 hours before the actual fight, which gives fighters time to rehydrate and eat before a fight. If one fighter cuts 20 pounds to make 145 pounds and the other doesn't cut at all, by the time of the actual fight the weight-cutter will outweigh his opponent by about 20 pounds, which is a very difficult-to-surmount advantage.

Chad always turns in a sick day in advance for Friday weigh-ins. When his supervisors ask how he could possibly know ahead of time that he's going to be sick, he invites them to come see for themselves. And it's true—when Chad's cutting weight, he's not a healthy human being. His cheeks are sunken, his eyes glazed, his mouth so dry he has trouble speaking. And we've discovered that the dehydration and malnutrition hinder his decision-making abilities. On days Chad's cutting weight, Brady makes it a point to stay home and babysit. The one time Brady didn't, he came home to find that Chad had gone to Costco and bought a 50-piece sushi platter and a DVD of *Couples Retreat*.

AT THE WEIGH-INS

The weigh-ins for Chad's upcoming fight are Friday at 6:00PM at The Jet Bar & Grill in Mill Creek, Washington.

The Jet is known as the place to go in the Mill Creek area if you're looking for a fight. A number of the bouncers are MMA fighters. Bouncing might be the only career that MMA actually helps. The Jet is exactly the sort of place that would host amateur MMA weigh-ins—and is the sort of bar where weigh-ins wouldn't seem completely bizarre to every customer—although I'm not sure what The Jet gets out of the arrangement.

I'm here with Chad, Brady, and a number of other people connected to the fights. We're sitting at bar tables without any drinks or food. There's an unknown delay for weigh-ins. Many of the people here are fighters who've been cutting weight—they're dehydrated, hungry, exhausted, and generally about as cranky as human beings can be. They're not particularly sociable. And it would seem rude to the fighters if the rest of us were talking and laughing and eating chicken wings. So we sit at bar tables mostly in silence. This is probably the least fun you can have in a bar.

When the weigh-ins finally start, it becomes clear that the people running the weigh-ins—I have no idea who they are—are attempting to turn them into a production, something that people would want to come watch. The scale is on the stage, someone is announcing fighters' names and weights, and there's even a photo op where opponents glare at each other and make fists. But the problem here is that the act of weighing a person on a scale to ensure that their weight is below a certain amount is irredeemably dull and not worth watching. There's no real drama, since the fighters surely weighed themselves before weigh-ins just to make sure they were on the mark. Really, the only remotely interesting aspect of weigh-ins is that the fighters do so in their underwear. What's interesting about it is that this is a very public place, and there are likely customers at The Jet here simply because they wanted to get a drink after work, customers who had no idea that they'd be viewing a bunch of unclothed, ripped yet severely dehydrated dudes.

Chad and Jonathan both make weight, and they have a stare-down photo op that'll be used in future *Ax Fighting* publicity. After we leave The Jet, Chad spends the next 24 hours rehydrating with water and Pedialyte while watching *Robocop* and *Jurassic Park III*. By mid-morning on Saturday he's back in full athletic and mental condition. Back at 165 pounds, he's as ready as he's going to be to avenge his one MMA loss.

CHAPTER 4

CHAD'S FIRST TITLE FIGHT

NINETEEN MONTHS AGO, RIGHT here at Edmonds Community College, Chad, in his amateur mixed martial arts debut, lost to Jonathan Moore by guillotine choke in the first round. Chad is now once again fighting Jonathan Moore to attempt to avenge his honor, take the *Ax Fighting* 145-pound title belt and all the honors it beholds, and entertain the 2,300 or so people gathered to watch the fights this evening.

In attendance tonight: Brady, Jake, our parents, my girlfriend, Chad's ex-girlfriend, Chad's best friend (also the ex-boyfriend of Chad's ex-girlfriend, but this is neither the time nor place to get into that), Chad's best friend's new girlfriend, and a handful of folks with whom we went to high school. In total there are about 14 people in our little clan, all here to watch Chad.

Tickets to tonight's event cost $25. The beneficiaries of *Ax Fighting*—Charlie, in particular—are making at least $350 from the goodwill of Chad's supportive family, friends, and younger brother who from the looks of it is the only person in the gymnasium who remembered to bring his Moleskine notebook.

As tonight's main event, Chad's fight is the last of 14 scheduled fights. This is about six fights too many for my taste and 12 too many for Jake's. To make things more interesting, Jake and I agree to bet a dollar on each fight. Jake loves gambling. Online poker, scratch tickets, friendly wagers on video games—Jake loves it. One time when Jake was nine, I found a toy store that sold win-ten-grand-every-time scratch tickets. They were fake, as anyone over age nine would realize. When I got home, I gave one to Jake, who immediately started scratching. Then he stopped, and he told Brady and me, "You guys, if I get one more dollar sign, I win ten-thousand dollars." We told him to call us when he had something interesting to say. He started scratching, and then within a few seconds he was running around the room screaming, "I won! I won!" Brady said he didn't believe him, and tried to grab the scratch ticket from Jake's hand, but Jake didn't want to let go, so Brady pulled and ripped the scratch ticket in half. Jake was shocked, and he asked us—on the verge of tears—if the ticket was still good. "No," we told him, "you can't turn in a ripped scratch ticket." After he cried for a few minutes we told him that the scratch ticket was fake all along, and we got him pretty good, huh?

Even after this, Jake still loves gambling.

Jake and I alternate who gets to pick his fighter. Jake's caveat is that we won't bet a dollar on Chad's fight. If it were my turn to bet I would bet on Chad, and then Jake would be in a terrible dilemma for an 11-year-old: he'd have to choose between rooting for his brother's safety and rooting for his dollar.

A man introduced as Ben sings "The Star-Spangled Banner." It is explained that Ben is a fighter, but he is not fighting tonight. He has a mohawk. I can't tell if he thinks the mohawk is ironic, or if he thinks it's retro, or if he's trying to make a self-conscious commentary on self-conscious commentaries. Ben, though, probably didn't think about any of these when he went for the mohawk, which seems endearing and refreshing. He seems honored that he's been given the opportunity to sing for all of us. He swings for the fences on the high notes. It is surprisingly okay.

FIGHT ONE

Apparently you don't have to qualify to fight in these things. If you want to fight, and someone else will fight you, then you can fight. You needn't be athletic or athletic-looking. Watching a pasty, flabby guy fight another pasty, flabby guy is about as exciting as watching a middle-school cross country meet.

FIGHT THREE

I learn from Jake that when you're on your back and roll over so that you're on top it's called an "Oompa Loompa." I find out later that this is not true at all. It's called an "Omoplata" and it's a little more complicated than that.

FIGHT FOUR

The fighter in the blue corner is wearing bike shorts, and before the fight he prances around the ring as though he's all jacked up on *Karate Kid* movies. He appears quite amped and ready to brawl to the death, as though he's been training for this moment for years and now finally has his chance to show the world what he's made of. He receives a quick and severe beating.

THE ZIPFIZZ GIRLS

After every three fights or so, the Zipfizz Girls come up into the ring. Zipfizz is apparently an energy drink, or, rather, a powder that transforms ordinary water into an energy drink. The Zipfizz Girls wear fishnet stockings and very little clothing. They're less attractive than the ring girls, yet they have the much tougher job of trying to seduce the audience into liking Zipfizz. I have it from Brady that Zipfizz tastes like "fizzy water piss with a hint of citrus." I haven't attempted to verify this.

What makes it worse is that the Zipfizz Girls' only task on stage is to throw out little sample tubes of Zipfizz, which no one really wants. At one point a tube of Zipfizz gets thrown back on stage. We're in the bleachers about 30 feet from the ring and thus out of Zipfizz range. I'm not sure what criteria were used to select the Zipfizz girls, but presumably they weren't chosen for their throwing arms.

Around the fourth fight Brady and I begin convincing Jake, who won the Wisdom Award last year at his private Christian school, that Zipfizz is awesome and that if he acquires Zipfizz he will be more acceptable in our eyes. We tell him the only way he can acquire Zipfizz is by going down to the ring and taking off his shirt. He asks us how close to the ring he needs to get. As close as he can get, we tell him, and it'll help if he swings his shirt over his head.

Jake trusts us. One time when he was seven, I was driving him somewhere when we pulled up to a stoplight next to a man driving a Hummer. "Rory," Jake said, "that guy has a small wiener." I asked him how he knew that. "Brady told me that people who drive Hummers have small wieners." To this day this is one of Jake's fundamental beliefs about the universe.

The next time the Zipfizz girls come on stage, Jake walks down the bleachers to the gym floor, just out of spotlight range. He raises his hands. The Zipfizz girls don't notice him. He looks up at us and we communicate that he needs to remove his shirt and swing it over his head. He steps closer to the ring, into the spotlight's circle, removes his shirt, and swings it over his head so everyone can see his 11-year-old nipples.

The Zipfizz girls throw Jake a tube of Zipfizz. He puts his shirt back on and returns to the bleachers. Our mother immediately confiscates the Zipfizz and begins sternly talking to Jake. She is not amused. Jake never gets to taste his Zipfizz. We later let Jake know that he is now more acceptable in our eyes and can hang out with us sometime.

TEAM RED LINE FIGHT

The photocopied paper that contains tonight's essential info—fighter names, weights, Zipfizz logo—states that one of the participants in this fight is from Team Red Line. He walks out to the fight with no fewer than nine people accompanying him. All of them are wearing white. They are waving red flags and seem very pumped up, angry even. It all looks way too much like the KKK. Jake says, "This guy has a pretty big posse."

The fighter from Team Red Line removes his robe. In large letters across the back of his shorts is written "TRL." Someone in the crowd yells, "Carson Daly!" The rest of the fight is un-noteworthy, and I'm not sure who won, although for some reason I wrote down that in mixed martial arts you are indeed allowed to smother.

FIGHT EIGHT

Someone in the audience uses—and possibly coins—the word "pussiest."

NOT RELATED TO ANY SPECIFIC FIGHT, BUT STILL IMPORTANT

Almost every fighter, when he/she throws a punch or kick, makes one of the following noises: *fwoot*, *shfit*, *hiff*, or *foof*. I assume fighters make these noises for the same mysterious reasons that tennis players grunt when they hit a ball. I must admit though that for the first two fights I attended I was under the impression that these were just the noises that punches made when they sliced through the air.

FIGHT NINE

Jake bets on an African American fighter to win this fight, and the African American does indeed win. Jake says, "I'm glad I like black people."

I've been betting on fighters based on sensible things—their win-loss records, which gym they fight at, how they've performed when I've watched them before. Jake's been betting based on Jake things—tattoos, color of shorts, shininess of muscles. When the second-to-last fight ends, Jake and I are even. (In case you're doing the math, one of the 13 fights was a tie.) I've learned tonight that sensible things don't perform any better than Jake things. Jake has learned that gambling is harmless and that you can bet on sporting events, or anything really, with no harm done and a good time had.

THE TITLE FIGHT

Jonathan Moore is 32, a nurse, and is married with a young child. I've been unable to verify any of these with anything resembling journalistic integrity, but Jonathan seems like a nice person, which makes it hard to view this as the ultimate battle of "good versus evil." He's no Team Iceland.

Also, like any good sibling, a small part of me hopes Jonathan lands a few solid punches. Chad's had it coming to him ever since the time when we were kids—I think he was 12 and I was 10—and had just watched the 3 *Ninjas* trilogy, and so naturally we decided to make pepper bombs out of coffee filters and anything we could find in our mother's spice drawer. Chad then somehow detonated one of these pepper bombs near my eyes. If Jonathan knees Chad in the kidney a few times I'll call it even.

The chorus for Chad's intro song is, *"I'm gonna knock you out. Momma said knock you out."* Our mom did not say this. The fight is scheduled for five three-minute rounds.

Round One. There's some get-to-know-you punching and arm-grabbing, which leads to what I'm going to call "The

Vigorous Man Hug," where Chad and Jonathan embrace each other and try to knee each other in the ribs and stomp on each other's toes but really don't do much of anything except wobble around the ring.

After a few minutes of this either Chad or Jonathan makes a noise that sounds like "huff-push-shoe-ee," and then Jonathan's head disappears. Chad is holding it under his left arm, by the neck. This is what is known as a guillotine, the exact same move Jonathan used to choke Chad out in their first fight, except now Chad is the one choking Jonathan out. This would be the perfect mirror ending, the most fitting way for Chad to avenge his loss.

Here's what various coaches and audience members advise Jonathan to do to escape the guillotine: "Peel that arm, peel it." "Push his chest out." "Come on." "Peel the arm." "Cross face, Jonathan." "Come on." "Hold the leg." "Peel it." "Come on." "Underhook the leg." "Come on." "Peel that arm."

And then, after one minute and ten seconds of restricted breathing, Jonathan somehow—I can't tell whether he uses the "Peel the Arm" or the "Come On"—slips his head out. The round soon ends. Jonathan later tells Chad that if it hadn't been a title fight he most likely would've tapped out and given Chad the fight.

I have no idea how these things are scored. I don't know if Chad got any points for choking Jonathan. I don't know if Chad accomplished anything in the first round, but in Jake's opinion Chad is winning.

Round Two. A few punches are thrown, and then Chad and Jonathan once again do The Vigorous Man Hug. Chad then picks Jonathan up and tosses him onto his back, with Chad on top. Jonathan is holding Chad too close for Chad to throw a punch. Jonathan also has Chad's legs wrapped up in his legs. Chad, with no other options, is smearing his hand across Jonathan's face, covering his mouth, and generally being a nuisance. Again, I don't know if you score points for this. This continues for the rest of the round and Chad, apparently frustrated that he's unable to throw a real punch, starts hammering Jonathan's face with his forearm bone. It is ineffective. The round ends.

Round Three. A few punches, another Vigorous Man Hug initiated by Chad, and then Jonathan tries to throw Chad to the ground, but Chad evades him using what our high school wrestling coach called "A Whizzer." (Origin of name unknown.) During this round we notice that Jonathan has a Mandarin character tattooed on his right shoulder, which according to my Mandarin-speaking girlfriend can be translated as either "Aspiration of Moral Virtue" or "Germany Ideal Volunteer." Around his belly button he has a tattoo of what looks like a shining sun. My Mandarin-speaking girlfriend says this is not a Mandarin character.

They hug and un-hug a bit, throw a few punches—nothing really connects—and then, when Jonathan goes for a big momma-said-knock-you-out punch, Chad ducks and tackles him, ending up on the ground in what's becoming their second favorite position, The "Horizontal" Vigorous Man Hug. This happens toward the end of the round, and before the bell rings Chad only has time to give Jonathan's face a good Dutch rub.

Round Four. More Vigorous Man Hugging.

Round Five. Someone in our little clan who understands the judging system explains that Chad will win if he avoids getting knocked out in this round. Although neither fighter has mangled the other in the first four rounds, Chad has clearly dominated.

So Chad does the same thing that's been working for him every round, which at this point is pretty boring. Jonathan's fans—sitting not too far from us—are booing Chad. They use derogatory terms. They tell him to stand up and fight him like a man, which would, of course, be silly.

This is, however, the round where Chad delivers the worst beating, relatively. For four minutes he consistently lands punches, shoulders, and even a sort of head-butt to Jonathan's face. Toward the end the announcer appears in the corner. He is wearing a floral-patterned shirt. The bell rings. It's soon announced that Chad has won by unanimous decision. Chad now has another trophy and a belt with a Frisbee-sized gold-color buckle. And now that Chad has avenged his loss, he's not quite sure what he'll do next.

CHAPTER 5

AMATEUR MMA GONE EVEN WILDER

WHAT CHAD DOES NEXT, it turns out, is fight in a novelty tag-team bout that won't affect his MMA career in any way. This tag-team fight will take place at an event called *Knockout at the Nile 2* at the Nile Shrine Temple in Shoreline, Washington. I drive by the Nile almost daily, yet I've never been able to figure out what it is. It looks like a country club and golf course, yet it calls itself a temple and seems to have some function beyond that of a normal country club. I've always suspected that the Nile is a front for a cult, a cult that hosts amateur mixed martial arts events.

Let me point out from the start that everything in this chapter is made possible by the United States Army. I broke the cardinal rule of journalism and brought only one pen tonight, a free pen acquired from a Westin Hotel. It stops working while I'm still in the parking lot. Do not use Westin

Hotel pens. They will fail you. I imagine that this reflects on Westin Hotels themselves.

Fortunately—and somewhat inexplicably—there's an Army recruitment table in the Nile's lobby area. While we're waiting in line to get in, the recruiter begins trying to recruit Brady. The recruiter asks Brady what he's been doing since high school and Brady tells him that he's been in college. He's been studying business at Seattle Pacific University, to be precise, which isn't exactly an Army feeder program.

The recruiter ignores me, although I too am a young, Army-eligible male. I'm beginning to worry that there's something about my appearance that says that I'm unfit to serve in the armed forces. It could be that I've been trying to rehabilitate a Westin Hotel pen with saliva.

I ask the Army recruiter for a pen from his jar of promotional Army pens. I tell the Army recruiter not to worry about recruiting me, that I'm not fit to serve in the armed forces. The recruiter nods and gives me the pen. It is a very nice pen.

I'm here tonight with Brady, Emily, my mom and dad, and someone named Garret. Jake is not here tonight. My parents are beginning to suspect that these MMA events—with their ring girls and people who have tattoos and likely grew up in apartments—might not be the best atmosphere for Jake. But my parents know that if they tell Jake he can't come, it'll come across as disapproval of his older brother and his chosen activities, and that it likely won't do any good because Jake will say that he just wants to come to spend time with his family, or some sly Jake thing like that. It's a terrible parenting dilemma, actually, exposing your kid to questionable surroundings versus telling your kid that his beloved older brother is himself part of the questionable surroundings. My parents have solved the dilemma for tonight by sending Jake to a youth-group activity that involves trampolines.

The fights are being held in a banquet room with chandeliers and a wall-sized sculpture thing that looks like a drafting compass trying to eat a right angle. That is, it looks like the sort of sculpture a cult would display.

A woman walks by drinking Red Bull from a can with a pink flexi straw. Directly above the cage is a disco ball large enough to contain an adult male, and not once during the night does it stop rotating. Padded folding chairs are set up in a flower petal pattern with the cage at the center. Garret gives me an unsolicited explanation of the phrase "elephant walk." The explanation is obscene and won't be reproduced here.

A woman who resembles my second grade teacher sings the national anthem. There is not an American flag in sight, nor anything remotely patriotic-looking, so instead of staring at a flag everyone stares at the cage. I get the unmistakable but unverifiable feeling that someone somewhere in the room is quietly singing along.

Tonight's fights take place in an actual cage. It's a hexagonal structure with padded posts at each corner, which obscure about 20 percent of tonight's action.

The third fight is something called a submission-wrestling match. There's no punching or kicking involved, but it's really nothing like any sort of wrestling I've seen. The "submission" part of the name would lead one to believe that the goal is to get your opponent to tap out by choking or bending him in an undesirable way.

The guys flop around, grabbing at each other. I have no idea what they're doing and whether they're doing it well. I get the feeling that everyone in the crowd is thinking what I'm thinking, *This is fucking Kafka-esque.* And by Kafka-esque, I mean it's weird and I don't get it. The match ends in a tie.

THE NILE SHRINERS

The concession stands are staffed by men wearing royal blue elastic baseball hats. Most of these men have gray hair, many have beards, and all are wearing white star badges that look like something a cartoon sheriff would wear. In age and attire these men seem like they don't really fit in with the crowd, so I assume they're a part of the Nile Shrine cult. I later find out that they're called Nile Shriners.

From my experiences tonight and from the Nile's website, here's what I know about Nile Shriners:

- Nile Shriners prefer to charge $5 for a plastic cup of beer.

- Nile Shriners use capital letters liberally and with no discernible pattern.

- Nile Shriners will sell a bottle of soda for $1 and a bottle of water of the same size for $2, and will fail to see the weirdness of this.

- Nile Shriners welcome ladies to become Nile Shriners, but in all instances the word "ladies" is used instead of, say, "women" or "females." There are no female Nile Shriners.

- Nile Shriners aren't categorically opposed to purple vests.

FIGHT FOUR: 135-POUND MMA

These fighters must be embarrassed. They wore the same outfit—black shorts with a single white stripe, no shirt. This is like showing up to the prom in the same dress as your best friend. Across the butt of their shorts is text that's completely illegible except for ".com."

After the first round a ring girl walks around the cage holding a sign with the number "2" on it, signifying that the next round is the second round. She's wearing four-inch heels, a not-entirely-slutty bikini, and can't be older than 20. She is pretty. The ring girl tradition is a carry-over from boxing, I believe. What's interesting, though, is that boxing matches can have up to 15 rounds, while the amateur MMA fights tonight have three rounds. For counting purposes, the ring girls aren't entirely necessary.

The girl walks around the ring, self-consciously shaking her general booty area. The eight Nile Shriners within eyeshot have all stopped what they're doing—one of them holding popcorn in mid-scoop—and are staring at the ring, heads swiveling to follow the girl. Each one of their mouths is slightly open.

FIGHT SIX

I miss most of the sixth fight, but my dad reports that this is the absolutely bloodiest fight he's seen in his whole life. He is unwilling or unable to provide a more detailed description or even offer any other adjectives besides "bloody."

I miss the fight because I'm in a back hallway conducting an investigation about the exact nature of the Nile Shrine Temple and the Nile Shriners that inhabit it. On the wall are framed newspaper articles, some of them decades old, all of them about the Masons. One of them mentions that 14 presidents have been Masons. No mention is made of why Masons would be interested in hosting amateur MMA fights in their ballroom.

I think it's fair to conclude that the Nile Shriners are some sort of Masonic sect. I don't know what the Masons are, actually. I know they're often associated with conspiracies. I know they were in that *Da Vinci Code* book. I know the Internet likely has more information on the Masons than I could possibly want, but I have a hunch that it's not worth the time.

I return to the main room and, under the guise of buying popcorn, ask one of the Shriners what they'll do with the proceeds from tonight's event. He explains that all proceeds from Nile Shrine events go toward helping burn victims. This sounds noble and altruistic. Exactly what a well-trained cult member would say.

CHAD'S TAG-TEAM FIGHT

Because this fight is supposed to be lighthearted and fun, it's been decided that the fighters cannot punch each other in the head. They can slap, but can't punch. This seems like the same sort of logic that's behind diet soda or non-alcoholic beer: when you try to make something healthy by removing the key ingredient, what's left is usually depressing and purposeless and still isn't healthy.

The announcer says, "Is two fighters in the cage enough? Sometimes I ask myself the same question." The program states that this fight features Team El Guapo San versus Team Extreme. I believe "El Guapo San" is Spanish for "The Handsome Saint." "Team Extreme" can only be the nomenclative work of CDextreme34.

The announcer introduces the fighters. In the red corner is Team El Guapo San: Chris "Chavez" Garcia and Landon "The Show" Showalter. In the blue corner is Team Extreme: Buck "The Slam" Bisbey and Chad "The Dastardly" Douglas.

Chad "The Dastardly" Douglas. I'm betting the announcer came up with that on the spot and has no idea what "dastard" actually means. It's likely he thinks it's a synonym for "bastard" and not a word that means "someone who avoids conflict in a cowardly manner," which is ironic in a way that, given the crowd, I decide to keep it to myself.

If you were a middle school boy at some point in the '90s, then the rules of tag-team fighting probably seem like one of those bits of knowledge you were born with. But for everyone else:

Tag-team fighting was popularized—and perfected—in the World Wrestling Federation. Two wrestlers wrestle or fight as usual, but each has a teammate waiting just outside the ring. If the wrestler inside the ring can somehow tag his teammate, the teammate can then enter the ring and take the first person's place. There's a brief and loosely regulated timeframe during these transitions where both members of a team can be in the ring at the same time, which means that at moments the fight is two-on-one or, less often, two-on-two.

It's clear from the start that the fighters aren't taking the fight seriously. The Slam tries a flying knee to the chest. The Dastardly slaps Chavez several times in the face. The Slam does a cartwheel thing that has no real purpose.

The whole thing is as boring as anticipated until two minutes into the first round, when The Dastardly gets choked out. Chavez arranges things so that he's on The Dastardly's back in a position best described as "doggy style."

Chavez wraps his arm around The Dastardly's neck, choking him until The Dastardly has to tap out.

The Dastardly apparently doesn't like to get choked out, much less choked out doggy style. He is pissed, and the fight abruptly becomes much less funny and much angrier. The slaps start to resemble closed-fist punches.

With a minute left in the fight, Chavez gets on The Slam's back, but then The Slam tags The Dastardly's foot. This allows The Dastardly to jump onto Chavez's back, and for a few seconds we have a Chavez sandwich with Team Extreme bread. According to tag-team rules, Chavez has to release The Slam, and by the time this happens The Dastardly has already locked in the same doggy-style choke Chavez used earlier. Chavez taps out, tying the score at one just before regulation time ends.

It appears that the referee and the announcer make up the overtime rules on the spot: all four fighters will rumble at the same time, *West Side Story* style. The fighters approach each other, and almost immediately the whole thing turns into a dogpile. Someone's arm is between someone's legs. An arm is wrapped around a head. A leg is flopping around on the mat.

It ends up that the winner is determined by that old whose-fist-is-on-top game. The Show ends up belly-down on the mat, The Slam on top of him, Chavez on top of The Slam, and The Dastardly on top of Chavez, which allows him to choke Chavez out doggy-style yet again, winning the match with what apparently is the only useful move in an amateur MMA tag-team fight.

Chad later points out that "doggy-style choke out" sounds obscene, and that the move is actually called a "rear naked choke."

145-POUND WOMEN'S MMA

One of the last fights of the night is a bout between Emma Bush and Sarah D'Alelio at 145 pounds. I'm pretty sure the announcer uses the phrase "girl-on-girl action." This makes it seem like it'll be exciting in a sorority-pillow-fight way, but it ends up being exciting for quite different reasons.

In the first 30 seconds it becomes apparent that these girls can punch. They punch hard, and often, and in the face. What these girls can't do, though, is block punches. Not once does either of them lift a glove to protect her face, nor do they try to bob or avoid punches in any way at all. It's a shootout: the girls take turns punching each other in the face. It is amazing. It looks like the winner will be the girl who can take the worst beating and still stay on her feet.

For two rounds I witness what has to be the most brutal fight ever held in a Mason Temple. In the third round Sara lands a punch directly on Emma's eye. Emma immediately puts a glove over her eye, but blood flows around it, down her face, and onto her white tank top.

I am concerned. I'm concerned that her eye has actually popped out of its socket. Blood seems to be squirting from her eye socket, as though it's been uncorked, where Emma's eye is the cork.

The referee blows the whistle, and Emma sits down. Her coaches tend to her. She removes her glove from her eye. Her eye is still in its socket, and blood covers most of her face.

The announcer says that Sara wins by technical knockout, which is a euphemism for "I beat you to such a bloody mess that you couldn't even see." Emma later goes to the doctor and finds out that the eyeball in question is now lodged three millimeters deeper into her skull.

CHAPTER 6

WRESTLING AND MMA

WHEN I WAS IN high school, I was a moderately successful wrestler on a very small, local, inconsequential level. What's important is that by any measure—win-loss record, state-tournament results, widely held public opinion—I was a better wrestler than Chad. When Chad was a senior and I was a sophomore, I qualified for the state tournament and he didn't. And my senior year I placed sixth at the state tournament. This isn't something I bring up at family gatherings. Not because it's obnoxious—it is—but because Jake, age 12, has already won a wrestling state championship and is a better wrestler than I was at 18, and any mention of my modest wrestling accomplishments will lead to Jake putting on his "Douglas State Champion" T-shirt and my dad turning on home videos of Jake wrestling. It's just not worth it.

I bring up wrestling because it's the one personal inroad I have for understanding MMA. High school wrestling has become a sort of gateway drug for local amateur MMA. The fight cards for local MMA events are stocked with names I remember from rival wrestling rosters, guys who used their wrestling experience as a starting point for taking up MMA after high school.

In some ways it makes sense. If you're a decent wrestler, you don't have many opportunities to use your wrestling skills after high school. Even if you wrestle in one of the few remaining college wrestling programs, after you graduate you're still left with an athletic skill that you rarely get to use. You can't go to a pickup-wrestling match at the playground and roll around for a while. There aren't rec leagues for playing grab ass with your buddies.

But in other ways it makes no sense at all. Wrestling is unpleasant and not much fun. This is a verifiable fact. If you want to actually compete as a wrestler, you have to cut weight, and you have to cut weight while attending classes and doing homework, and you have to do it two or three times a week, getting so dehydrated that your urine turns the color of orange soda. All unpleasant. Wrestling is the only sanctioned high school sport where you can catch herpes. Not fun. High school wrestling is the only reason I've ever ran stairs with a 106-pound person on my back. Unpleasant. High school wrestlers have, reportedly, been urinated on in the shower. Not fun. And then sometimes you end up wrestling someone so impossibly better than you that they literally throw you around the mat for 45 seconds before pinning you in a move where your hips and knees are flat against the mat but your torso is twisted so that your shoulder blades are also touching the mat. Again, unpleasant.

Sure, you get a whiff of actual fun when you win a big match or have a nice *Breakfast Club* chat with your teammates, but then sometimes you lose a match to a kid you should've beat, sometimes you lose a match to a kid with no legs, and sometimes you have a guy on your team whose jacket always smells like cat urine and when asked if his cat peed on it he says, unflinchingly, "Yes," and when asked why he didn't get rid of the jacket he says it was his favorite jacket, and when asked why he didn't just stop his cat from peeing on the jacket he says that it was his cat's favorite jacket too.

So the question here is why, given all this unpleasantness—especially the several types of urine-based unpleasantness—why would anyone even want to wrestle in the first place?

I can only vouch for my personal reasons for wrestling from 6th to 12th grade. Some of these reasons were apparent at the time, but others didn't become clear until much later in life.

At the time I knew I enjoyed being moderately good at something—and wrestling is one of the few sports a 5 feet 8 inches, 140-pound mediocre athlete can be moderately good at—and there was an ascetic pleasure in being the sort of person who went to wrestling practice instead of going home and eating Cheerios and watching *Oprah*, as our coach put it. I liked having friends from the team and having some sort of identity as a wrestler. These are all just the basic reasons that anyone does any high school sport. It's likely that another sport would've served these purposes just as well.

The only reason I had for choosing wrestling over other sports—namely swimming (it's at the same time as wrestling, and I'd grown up on swim team)—was the very miserableness itself. I took immense private pride in how unpleasant wrestling was, how I'd gone to intensive wrestling camp where there were four practices a day, how I could lose five pounds of sweat in a single practice, how (reportedly) wrestlers from our team who went on to join the Air Force said (reportedly) that Air Force boot camp was nothing compared to a decent Cascade High School wrestling practice.

MMA fighters might have a similar pride in the miserableness of their sport. Chad has said as much, how cool it is to go into work with black eyes, the feeling of knowing you do something no one else would even dream of doing. He usually mentions *Fight Club* in this little speech, and as a strict rule I disregard any parallels that fighters draw between MMA and *Fight Club*, since the first rule of MMA is that you tell everyone about MMA and that you probably have a pro MMA fight coming up.

But there were other reasons I wrestled in high school, ones I didn't acknowledge until later in life. I think these reasons might get us closer to figuring out why some wrestlers take up MMA after high school. To get into these reasons, we're going to have to start with my Overgeneralized Theory of High School.

By most adult standards, even the coolest high school student is an absolute loser. He lives at home. He's unemployed or works a minimum-wage job. He's required to be somewhere during working hours but does not get paid for it. If he drives a nice car it's a nice car his parents own. He really doesn't have anything interesting to talk about or any original ideas or anything to offer society except a promise that he'll go to college or get a job and in five or six years maybe he won't be such a complete waste of space and resources. You take your coolest 17-year-old and call him a 27-year-old and he becomes a huge loser.

And in high school, you're a huge loser at the time in life when you're both least equipped to deal with being a loser and most concerned with whether or not you are a loser.

As it relates to high school sports, this theory posits that sports distract some students from what would otherwise be a soul-crushing awareness of their unmitigated loserhood. When you're in high school, sports are one of the few things you can be pretty good at by adult standards. Of course, even a decent high school basketball player would get destroyed in the NBA, but that same decent basketball player is probably better than the vast majority of the adult population, simply by nature of being young and in his athletic prime and having lots of time to devote to basketball. So, in high school if you have any knack at all for sports you can focus on this one area where you're verifiably not a huge loser while meanwhile developing the personality and skills that will someday make you less of a loser in the adult world. And for some, this high school glory will become the peak moment of an entire lifetime.

Most of us, by the time we're in our early twenties a) have tiny things to offer the world by way of our professional skills or our personality as a whole and b) are aware that, yes, we're still losers, but not as much as we used to be, and that accepting that you're sort of a loser and working to become less of one is just part of adult life. And so by the time we're out of high school or college or an early-twenties post-college slump we no longer need the shelter of athletics to protect us from the realities of adult life.

(This theory as stated here doesn't account for the huge number of high school students who don't participate in athletics and really only focuses on a middle-to-upper-class subsection of high school students in the United States. I'd venture to say that other activities can play the same role—drugs, marching band, theatre—and that a small number of students have psyches of steel and can withstand that crushing awareness of what losers they are, but that's outside the scope of this inquiry, and furthermore I am not your guidance counselor.)

I'm willing to say that this theory accounts for the big reason I wrestled in high school, and it also explains why I don't miss wrestling. I don't need it. Not that I'm the paragon of adult maturity, but, like many adults, I get that I will always be something of a loser, and I also have a life and dog that I fucking own and a job where someone values my contribution so much that they hand me cash—and even health insurance, lest sickness deprive the company of my invaluable contributions—in exchange for my time, so much cash that I don't have to give the smallest of shits about Free Slurpee Day because I can afford a Slurpee any damn day of the year.

So, let's consider two things. First, let's posit that my reasons for wrestling are common among wrestlers. Second, let's posit that the difference between the actual sports of MMA and wrestling is merely one of degree, i.e., that MMA is just a more ultimate version of wrestling, and whatever someone wanted out of wrestling they could get in greater doses from MMA. Again, I'm just trying to use wrestling as some sort of personal inroad to understanding MMA fighters. I don't know whether any of these statements are true. But let's say they are. If that's the case, then what's the difference between a high school wrestler, like I once was, and a high school wrestler who after high school took his skills to MMA?

Well, one of them (the MMA fighter) is an adult. That answer might seem obvious or stupid or circular, but it's also true. Wrestling is a sport you do in high school or maybe college, and MMA is typically a sport you do as an adult.

But it's not just that. MMA, like wrestling, is one of the few sports an average athlete can be pretty good at. And MMA is also the only sport I can think of where an average adult athlete, with training and good old perseverance, can receive the same levels of attention as high school athletes do. You don't have to be an elite athlete to compete in MMA and have all your friends and family and a lot of people you don't even know spend their Saturday night watching you compete under an actual spotlight, and these people may even respect you or consider you a good athlete or at least consider you a curiosity worthy of a few minutes' consideration.

Therefore, it might be the case that some fighters take up MMA in part because it protects them from the awareness of what a loser they still are, much the way wrestling may have protected them in high school.

I don't mean to extend my Overgeneralized Theory of High School into a Condescending Theory Regarding MMA Fighters. Most adults are still losers, one way or another, and it'd be very tough to say that amateur MMA fighters are bigger losers than the general adult population. And neither do I want to say that MMA fighters are less equipped to deal with the reality of being sort of a loser. It's more a matter of preference. An ex-wrestler turned MMA fighter differs from someone like me—an ex-wrestler turned no way in hell would I ever do MMA—in that they prefer to go through all that time and pain and stress so that they can get a respite, a little vacation, from the relentless and pretty much lifelong awareness that they are in some degree a loser. An hour or so on a Saturday night every few months where people pay money to watch you perform and where, even if you lose, people still think what you just did was awesome and they acknowledge that you could kick their ass, and if you win, you just defeated another human being in a no-holds-barred fight, and for doing so you receive the cheers of a crowd, you're given a trophy or maybe even a belt, and your photo is taken with decent-looking girls who are wearing two-piece swimsuits indoors with nary a body of water in sight. Doesn't that sound kind of nice? I think any of us can understand why that sounds kind of nice.

CHAPTER 7

ABOUT AS FAR BEHIND THE SCENES AT AN MMA EVENT AS YOU COULD POSSIBLY WANT TO GO

I'M BACK AT EDMONDS Community College tonight to try to find the rest of the answer to that why-would-anyone-do-MMA question. I'm also here because I can get in for free. Chad's coaching fighters at tonight's *Ax Fighting* event, which means that if I arrive early and walk in with him I can avoid purchasing a $30 ticket and can pretend I have a backstage press pass. I'm hoping to get a behind-the-scenes look at the amateur mixed martial arts world. I want to see how fighters mentally prepare in the hours before a fight. I want to learn what's really going on in their heads when they think about fighting another person in an almost-no-rules fight, and what motivates them to do it.

Right now I'm watching a balding referee explain the rules of amateur mixed martial arts. Or, rather, he's explaining the house rules for tonight's event, *Ax Fighting 29*. Apparently

MMA rules vary slightly depending on the venue, as though it's Gin Rummy or Kick the Can.

"There will be no biting," the ref says, "and no eye gouging. There will be no fish hooking, no throat strikes, no head stomping. There will be no throwing your opponent out of the ring." The ref says that at the last fight he officiated someone was thrown out of the ring onto the gymnasium floor four feet below, so he thought he should emphasize this no-throwing-people-out-of-the-ring rule.

"There will be no striking in the spine or the back of the head." A fighter asks what is meant by "back of the head." The ref defines it as the area on the back of the head between the ears and above the neck.

"There will be no spiking anywhere on the head." Everyone else seems to know what spiking means. "There will be no kicking in the nards." Some of these are technical MMA terms. "No foot stomps." You can punch the foot but the referee doesn't foresee any circumstances where you would want to do so.

"If you're knocked out," the ref says, "the fight's over. If you're on your stomach getting bombs dropped on you, it's over. If you start yelling like a baby or a maniac, it's over. If you get a bad cut, the fight is over."

You're allowed to have three people in your corner. Two of them are permitted to enter the ring between rounds. You can put Vaseline on your face—it helps prevent fight-ending gashes—but nowhere else. When you tape your hands underneath your gloves, you cannot tape over the front of your knuckles. When I inquire about this later, I'm told that any padding on the hands—whether it's athletic tape or the thin six-ounce MMA gloves—enables the puncher to throw harder punches without concern for his hand's well-being. Having less padding is actually better for the person being punched, not for the puncher. Apparently hand injuries are to MMA what knee injuries are to soccer.

Chad isn't fighting tonight. In fact, Chad hasn't fought since his tag-team fight five months ago—which hardly counts—so it's been almost seven months since Chad's last real fight. Chad doesn't have an injury or really any reason for not fighting except that the right opponent hasn't come along. When you're toward the top of the amateur MMA heap, you have fewer options for opponents. Chad's not yet really ready to take a professional fight, but he also doesn't want to waste his time and risk injury—or a fluke loss—fighting a much lesser amateur fighter. Chad needs someone at his weight who has a solid record and wants to fight Chad. Right now, there's really no one in the greater Seattle area who meets these criteria, or so I'm told. There are a few up-and-coming guys and a few more recovering from injuries, but until one of them is ready Chad has to take a sabbatical from fighting or else go out of state to find an opponent, which doesn't happen too much at the amateur level. So, in the meantime, he's training and on occasion—like tonight—coaching.

When the ref is done with the rules, the fighters are dismissed to begin preparing themselves for their fights. Half of the fighters are sent to one prep room, and their respective opponents are sent to a separate prep room.

The prep room I'm in is just an aerobics room with yoga posters on the wall and a half-dozen stationary exercise bikes chained together with a bike lock. I don't see how anyone prepares for a fight in this atmosphere. The other prep room is both a men's locker room and a restroom.

A group of fighters is having a debate that ends in agreement that the apex of Jim Carrey's career was *Ace*

Ventura: Pet Detective. They then debate whether Mike's Hard Lemonade is an acceptable breakfast beverage. No definitive conclusion is reached. Several of the fighters are drinking water from gallon milk jugs. Someone is accused of grinding up and then snorting his daily vitamins. A coach tells one of his fighters to "go potty."

"I don't have to go," the fighter says.

"Go make yourself go," the coach says.

The fighter leaves to go potty.

I note that the night's program uses the word "becomming." The program also has the logos of *Ax Fighting's* sponsors: Emerald City Smoothie, Zipfizz, Tropical Tan, and what looks like the letter F.

A coach somewhere in the room gives his fighter pre-fight wisdom in a surprisingly spot-on Yoda voice. It's now 6:15 p.m. We have an hour and 45 minutes until the fights. I find someone to stamp my hand so I can re-enter for free, and I leave to go get dinner. One of the fighters commissions me to buy him a bottle of Captain Morgan Rum for post-fight use.

Shortly before the fights start I return and sit in the back row of bleachers. Since I'm by myself and have a few minutes, I start doing some amateur MMA philosophizing in my notebook.

Whenever I ask MMA fighters what exactly attracts them to fighting, their answers usually involve the words "rush," "dude," and "adrenaline." This is fine and almost descriptive, but it doesn't really explain what fighters get from MMA that they couldn't get from skateboarding or a rowdy afternoon on the community swimming pool diving board. When asked how MMA is different from other sports, fighters usually say something along the lines of "it's not like anything else I've ever done."

Before I get into this, let me note that playing grab-ass wrestling in the stands is apparently the MMA version of bringing your glove to a baseball game.

So, the issue here is that MMA fighters—the only people who could explain what it's like to voluntarily fight in an almost no-rules fight—are generally ineloquent in their explanations of what attracts them to MMA. Which leaves someone like me with no way of knowing what it's like to lie on my back in front of a thousand people and have fists rain on my cheekbones.

For most amateur sports—from bowling and kickball leagues to long-distance running to snowboarding—participants can only really expect small payoffs. Things like physical fitness, camaraderie, the solid feeling of progressing at something measurable. Small-scale self-improvement. MMA offers all of these things, and since it's one of the most extreme amateur sports, it offers all these things in bulk. But it's still tough to accept that any amount of community or fitness—or even the fleeting attention of a few thousand people, or a short respite from the awareness of what a loser you are—could possibly be worth getting punched in the skull again and again.

Here is one thing I suspect: for fighters, getting punched in the skull is its own reward. This might be what fighters are trying to get at when they say that MMA "isn't like anything else." If you're a fighter, you can spend your day knowing that you do something, something extreme, that none of the people at your day job will ever do. It's a good feeling, a basic feeling: the feeling of being special.

But there's probably a little bit more to it than that. Giving or receiving a beating requires all your entire mental and physical attention. It might be that when you're fighting another person—or even sparring with another person during training—that you get to take a short break from your life and thoughts and self and be totally occupied with something else. For some people, maybe for a lot of people, that short break from yourself might be worth any number of skull punches.

The fights start, and my philosophizing ends for the moment. A few rows in front of me there's a suspicious exchange involving a small black pouch and a bag of Sour Patch Kids.

FIGHT ONE

The first fight tonight features a guy I'm going to call Purple Mohawk fighting a guy I'm going to call Brian. Purple Mohawk throws Brian to his back and then bends Brian so that Brian's feet are behind Brian's ears. Purple Mohawk tires of this and lifts Brian up only to slam him back to the ground.

MMA announcers and fans use the phrase "raining punches" often enough that it's prone to lose its meaning. I believe the image it was originally meant to evoke was that of a poor little man stuck outside in a rain shower, one in which each raindrop is a little fist pounding on his face, and each time a fist goes by the man's ear it hovers for a moment to whisper "you will amount to nothing in life."

Purple Mohawk rains punches on Brian until he's no longer able to defend himself.

FIGHT TWO

In the second fight, in round two, someone gets kicked in the testicles. The announcer explains that when an accidental groin strike occurs the groin-strikee can take a recovery break of up to five minutes.

The groin-strikee's pain is visible—it appears that his testicles have retreated to somewhere near his lungs and he's trying to will them back to their proper place. At the same time, he's grinning like it's Christmas morning. He later ends up losing.

FIGHT THREE

We're now on fight three. At one point during this fight one guy is on his hands and knees, struggling to stand up, and the other guy, standing next to him, winds up and kicks him in the ribcage. This is now the image I'll get in my mind whenever someone uses the phrase "kick him while he's down." I believe this is against the rules, but nothing is done about it. Someone in the crowd yells, "Don't be a girl. Don't be shy."

I'm sitting in the back row of the stands by myself, scribbling all this in my notebook. I'm beginning to get odd looks. I'm afraid people are thinking I'm the sort of person who comes to amateur mixed martial arts events to update his "feelings" journal. I walk down and watch the fights from the standing room section on the gym floor.

When the Zipfizz girls start coming onto the stage, Chad invites me into the aerobics room where some fighters are preparing for their fights while others are recovering from their fights. Charlie is saying something regarding someone who's "not going to lose to a guy with narcolepsy."

The fighters who've already fought are unwrapping their gloves and icing various wounds. The fighters who haven't fought are pacing around, listening to music. Chad and his friend Buck are discussing how a lot of fighters get amped up too early. Buck says, "That shit wears me out."

Further philosophizing: no one ever brings it up, but it seems interesting to me that in amateur mixed martial arts, there's no drug testing. In professional MMA, they have mandatory drug testing for all fighters. In the '00s, there were a few incidents of UFC fighters testing positive for illegal performance-enhancing drugs. A few fighters were shamed, a few suspended, but it generally wasn't as big of a deal as it was with baseball or cycling. My personal suspicion is that when people looked at the fighters who had been accused of doping they thought, *Yeah, no shit.*

From a certain angle it seems silly to even discuss amateur MMA and performance-enhancing drugs. Few amateur sports have drug tests, after all. And amateur MMA isn't exactly a factory producing the next multi-millionaire UFC fighter. There's not a lot to be gained, and there's a lot to lose—most fighters seem to value their fighting community, and it'd bring a lot of shame on the sport and on a fighter's gym if they were caught doping.

But it might be somewhat naïve to assume that absolutely no amateur MMA fighters use performance-enhancing drugs. Some of them have aspirations of becoming pro fighters, and some have aspirations of being total meathead badasses. Some just really want to win. And without any sort of drug testing, your chances of getting caught are very low indeed. If there's something about MMA that's so powerful and attractive that fighters are willing to get punched in the skull, then surely a few fighters would be willing to take performance-enhancing drugs to get from MMA whatever it is they're trying to get.

BACK TO THE FIGHTS

These fighters weighed in at 215 pounds, which is a lot of man flesh. One of the fighters comes out to a song featuring the lyrics *"rat-a-tat-tat-tat."* His opponent's song features a ukulele. I think we all know who we're rooting for.

Rat-a-Tat immediately starts throwing wild punches. Each time he connects, someone in the audience yells, "Boom!" Rat-a-Tat throws Ukulele to the ground, sits on top of him, and punches him in the skull. He does this nine more times in the first round. It's brutal.

Between rounds a man walks past me wearing a formfitting, ribbed white tank top. Under this formfitting, ribbed white tank top, just above his nipple area, is the unmistakable outline of a flask.

Ukulele's face now has more blood visible than skin. He can't honestly believe he has any chance of winning this fight. Fighters have an actual towel they're allowed to throw to forfeit a match. This is a respectable option. It usually happens about once a night, and right now seems like a good time for it.

And yet Ukulele, with no real chance of winning and a high chance of a severe beating, goes on to fight another round. It's a special moment, for me at least, and I'm hoping that Ukulele, just as I am, is reaching back to his sophomore English class to recall the words of Atticus Finch, "(Courage is) when you know you're licked before you begin but you begin anyway and you see it through no matter what."

Ukulele then spends two rounds having his face smothered by 215 pounds of man flesh, and then loses.

I have no way to prove this, but I suspect that one of the things that attracts fighters to MMA is that at any moment during a fight they could suddenly experience the worst pain a person can experience. It seems like that would leave refreshingly little room for self-consciousness. I suspect that the moment a fighter pauses to think, *I'm in a gymnasium in TapouT shorts participating in an amateur mixed martial arts event and looking quite cool*, that's probably the moment he gets his kneecap stomped. I later run these thoughts by a fighter who responds, "Yeah, totally."

In the next fight a guy gets his skull battered against the ground. He ends up lying on his back while the other guy, from a standing position, rains punches on his face. This can't be pleasant. The back of his head is against the ground. Normally when someone gets punched, his head can whiplash into the air. Now there's nowhere for his head to go. It's sort of like curb stomping, upside down, with a fist. This goes on for an entire round.

FLAT TOP

There is a man who appears to be here tonight solely to jump onto the end of fighters' posse trains and, once there, to look at the crowd and raise the roof. He's an African American man with a flat top haircut currently dyed pink. He calls himself Flat Top. I've seen him fight before—he's an excellent fighter—but for some reason he hasn't been fighting lately.

Flat Top is a minor legend around the north Seattle suburbs amateur MMA world. Not necessarily because of his fighting prowess, but more for his extracurricular behavior. Someone told me that they saw Flat Top bring his infant to the gym, set it in the corner, and then work out for two hours. Someone else told me that he played poker next to and won substantial amounts of money off of Flat Top at the

Red Dragon Casino in Mountlake Terrace. I've heard reports that Flat Top drives around in a silver Mustang convertible with a "Flat Top" sticker across the windshield. Eyewitnesses report that they've seen Flat Top at the Everett Mall wearing a short-sleeved surfing rash guard. I once saw Flat Top knock out his opponent in a fight by kicking him repeatedly in the thigh. Regarding Flat Top, Chad says that mixed martial arts is the first thing he's really been good at, and it has been nothing but a positive thing in his life—it's given him a community, taught him discipline, and helped him rein in his all-around unique brand of goofiness.

This is the last fight I ever see Flat Top at. After tonight, he simply disappears from the MMA scene.

We're now on fight eight. The fighter I bought the rum for is walking around with a bottle of Coca-Cola. It should be noted that quite a few fighters begin celebratory or consolatory binge drinking almost immediately after their fights.

At one point the actual fight is stopped for what the announcer calls "a technical difficulty." It's pretty obvious what the technical difficulty is, so after a few moments the announcer goes ahead and says it, "In case you're wondering, the technical difficulty is that there's blood all over the place."

The final fight is a kickboxing match. In the fifth round one of the fighters lands a roundhouse kick on the other guy's face, but instead of connecting foot to face he connects shin to face. The shin is the closest thing the human body has to a baseball bat. After this, the towel is thrown. Every fighter in the room saw this happen. They've probably seen worse. And yet these fighters still continue to step into the cage, knowing that they might just get clubbed with a shin. There's something about MMA that's worth the risk. It might be the risk itself. It could be all the shelter-from-loserhood stuff mentioned previously. It could be that there's a simple joy in simple aggression. Perhaps something so silly and simple that I'm overlooking it. I'm betting that for most fighters it's a mix of all these and probably some other reasons I have yet to discover, and I'm also betting that, whatever it is, the rest of us won't ever be able to fully understand it.

CHAPTER 8

INTRODUCING BILLY WALKER

CHAD STILL HASN'T TAKEN another fight. It's been more than seven months since his title fight against Jonathan Moore. He's planning on fighting again, and is more or less obligated to, if he wants to defend his belt and retain his good name in the amateur mixed martial arts world. I'm beginning to suspect that it's not just a lack of opponents that's keeping Chad from fighting. I suspect that Chad's being somewhat picky about who he fights. It's almost inevitable that Chad will have to take a really tough fight, and I also suspect that he's grown fond of winning all the time.

In some ways, following an amateur athlete isn't nearly as gratifying as following a professional sport. Amateur athletes are under no obligation to compete on a regular schedule or to continue competing at all. It's quite unlike, say, Major League Baseball, where the massive amount of money involved almost requires that all relevant parties do whatever's necessary to make some sort of baseball season happen every year. And everyone makes sure that that season is narratively satisfying; the baseball season is structured in a way that guarantees some sort of satisfying narrative. Every year one team will have to endure the trials of the full season, battle through worthy contenders in the playoffs, and finally defeat another team in a climactic best-of-seven-game World Series. Depending on who you're rooting for, the winning team might be a hero or an antihero, but either way you'll at least have a structurally sound story. A beginning where the characters and teams are introduced and the plot gets going, a middle where it becomes clear where the real conflict is and which teams will actually become contenders, and an end where the action intensifies and teams drop one-by-one until only one team remains standing. It's as though the people running Major League Baseball—or any of the other major U.S. sports leagues—actually paid attention to the plot-structure part of their college Shakespeare classes.

You're not guaranteed this sort of story structure with amateur MMA. If you're following a specific fighter, you might know when their career begins, but you have no idea what part of it is the middle and what part of it is the end. With Chad, for example, for all I know his fight with Jonathan Moore was the climax of his career, yet at the time I thought it was just a step toward more important fights. Even now, seven months later, I don't know whether that fight was the beginning, middle, or end of his career. This sort of uncertainty isn't the stuff of good storytelling, and it frustrates the part of me that was raised on professional sports leagues and Disney sports movies.

Yet what amateur MMA lacks in plot structure it more than makes up for with its characters. Since Chad is my brother, I obviously know him much better than I could ever know a real professional athlete, and that gives his athletic career a richness and drama that you just can't get from anything that's televised. But even other fighters—like Billy Walker, Chad's training partner—are pretty much the definition of normal people, and if you're so inclined you can ask them a few half-assed journalistic questions and learn enough about them that you'll want to spend your Saturday evening at an MMA event seeing how they do at their fight.

So, tonight I'm going to an event called *Knockout at the Nile 4*—which takes place yet again at our neighborhood Masonic Lodge—to watch Billy fight for the Cage Wars 135-pound title belt. Here's what you would know about Billy if you'd only met him a few times and hadn't tried and failed to conduct a journalistic interview with him: he's an electrician, he's an adult male that continues to go by "Billy," he has a tattoo of a sunshine-moon graphic three inches above his left nipple, and he really loves blue trucks. That alone is enough for me to like Billy and care about his MMA career.

But if you attempt putting Billy through anything that could possibly be construed as an interview you'll learn a few things about him that give his MMA career some depth. He's 28, and he's been fighting for three and a half years. Billy's mom died when he was five, and his dad lost custody of Billy, and wasn't really around until Billy was 12. He went to boarding school in Nebraska and then, when he was an adult, he came out to Seattle because he thought there'd be more opportunity there.

The reason this is interesting to me is that the guys at Charlie's Combat Club represent one of the best communities that Billy's been a part of. Charlie's like a big brother to him, Billy says—like a mentor. And Billy says that fighting has mellowed out his aggression issues quite a bit, since he now has a place to take out his aggression. And—still paraphrasing Billy—even though MMA has made Billy much tougher, getting regular beatings at practice and in competition has made him much less arrogant and less prone to start extracurricular fights. In a lot of ways, MMA has been a net positive for Billy.

Not in all ways, though. Billy is also the father of two girls, ages two and eight. He's been divorced from their mother for about a year now. Billy says that MMA probably "played a factor in my divorce, put a wear on my girls." Part of this is that Billy trains six days a week, two to four hours a day. Billy says that most people in his life are pretty supportive of MMA but his ex-wife "doesn't like it."

I miss the first two fights tonight because I'm trying to find a way into the building that doesn't require a $30 general admission ticket. I consider it a moral affront for a religious organization, however cultish it might be, to charge $30 for a sporting event that doesn't involve Pelé joyriding Secretariat through Wimbledon.

My attempts to sneak in turn out to be futile. Two or three old Masons are guarding every possible entrance, and after I circle the building twice I lose my moral indignation and simply feel dumb that I can't outsmart a bunch of old men wearing purple hats. I end up calling Chad, who's helping coach Billy tonight, and he somehow finagles a pass for me from another coach.

In the center of the room is a cage, surrounded by folding chairs 15 rows deep. All the chairs are full, and in the open space behind them is a standing mass of people. I soon have sweat in all my most personal places. There is no good place to stand. I haven't even been able to find a program explaining who's fighting who at what weight.

FIGHT THREE

The first fight I catch is between two guys who simply won't punch each other. They circle around the ring shoving each other, like a reenactment of every fight that ever happened at my middle school. During the second round I realize that it's some sort of wrestling match, which explains the lack of punching. And this wrestling match, unlike every wrestling match I've seen at MMA events, actually ends in a victory. The flabby, pasty wrestler chokes out the tattooed, spray-tanned guy. It's a victory for the universe as a whole.

FIGHT FOUR, BY THE NUMBERS

Number of times someone behind me and to my right yells, "Find your rhythm!": 2.

Number of times above-mentioned faceless voice yells, "Hands up!" to his favored fighter: 13.

Number of times the fighter puts his hands up in response to one of these admonitions: 2.

Number of ring girls who, while booty-shaking around the ring between rounds, receive 1970s-construction-site-style catcalls: 1.

Estimated age of said ring girl: 17.

Number of ring girls who don't really receive catcalls at all: 2.

Number of spit buckets used between rounds to receive a gooey substance unlike any saliva a human would produce under normal circumstances: 1.

Final score of fight: 29–28, 28–29, 29–28.

Estimated number of audience members who have any idea what that means: 14, which doesn't include me.

The losing fighter stomps out of the cage, and I don't need to follow him to know that he's going to do some top-drawer little-league-style bitching about "bad calls" and "fuck this" and "stupid judges."

FIGHT FIVE

The first fighter has his hair braided into two sad pigtails that look like how Pippi Longstocking would wear her hair if Pippi Longstocking was an angry young African American male. On his way out to the cage he stops for a moment to scowl at the audience.

The second fighter—whose name, according to the program I've finally obtained, is Wallid—is wearing the exact outfit my dad wears when he goes jogging: a hooded sweatshirt, mesh shorts, and ASICS running shoes. Wallid gets slightly lost as he jogs to the cage but eventually makes it.

It appears that Angry Longstocking has an erection. It could be that his shorts are designed to create a bulge near where his penis is located, but I don't know why anyone would construct or buy shorts with this feature.

The fight begins. It's not long until Angry Longstocking and Wallid get into a position we're going to call "London Bridge is Falling Down." Here's what happens in LBIFD: Angry Longstocking is standing up, sort of crouched over. The mysterious bulge is still there, if you're keeping track. Wallid is belly up on the floor and has his legs wrapped around Longstocking's neck. I don't know how they got into this position, but here we are.

Longstocking stands to his full height so that the back of Wallid's head is three feet off the floor. Wallid's hang-onto-his-neck tactic seems ill-advised at the moment, but he hangs on, even though he has to know what's coming. Longstocking swings his whole upper body toward the ground, hammering the back of Wallid's head into the cage floor.

This is a good place to point out that the cage floor isn't particularly soft. It's about as forgiving as kitchen linoleum.

Wallid still doesn't let go. Longstocking stands up and again drops Wallid's head to the floor. He does this three or four more times—it's brutal—and then the ref blows the whistle, ending the fight. It is then announced that Wallid Mahggob—yes, he of what must be a grade-one concussion—has won the fight.

What happened, I later learn, was that Wallid was using his legs to choke Angry Longstocking. Each time Longstocking slammed Wallid's head to the ground, Wallid tightened his hold around Longstocking's neck until, finally, after much violence, Longstocking could no longer breathe and had to tap out.

I'm impressed, and wondering if this says something about human perseverance through pain, about sticking to your strategy even when your tactics seem doomed, and then I notice that Pippi's erection—or whatever it is—is still present. Wallid, in an unrelated gesture, raises the roof.

FIGHT SIX

Fight six is between two fighters who've never fought before. During this fight I notice that if you fought at any point in the evening you apparently have the right to spend the rest of the night shirtless.

The rather unentertaining fight ends in a split decision, and there are somehow people in the audience who care enough to boo the judges. The announcer tells them to leave the fights for the ring, that "this is not the place to play tough guy." I disagree. If there's anywhere that's the place to play tough guy, it's an amateur mixed martial arts event. Everyone but me paid $30 for the privilege.

INTERMISSION

I have an ongoing quest to interview a ring girl. I have so many questions: How does a girl go about becoming a ring girl? Are they paid? Do they have to apply? Try out? Interview? Have they always dreamed of being a ring girl? How old are they, really?

But any possible start to an interview would seem like a feeble pick-up attempt, "Good evening, could I ask you a few probing questions and write down the answers with my creepy red pen in my notebook that's mysteriously moist?" No, all the good journalistic approaches have been ruined by sleazy men. I'll need to craft a different strategy.

In a hallway outside the cage-room proper I witness a man trying to let a friend sneak in the back door. He receives the wrath of three old men in purple hats barking "hey" at him. It is terrifying. When I return to the venue proper someone yells, "I'm never buying Zipfizz again!" It appears the announcer has changed T-shirts.

FIGHT EIGHT

I'm mentioning this rather dull fight only because it helped me pin down why the $30 ticket price gets under my skin. One of the fighters, Colton, has a cheering section of about 19 people, most of whom look to be mom and aunt-types and 40-year-old men wearing sunglasses. That is, it looks like his whole extended family has turned out to support him. Some of them have brought signs saying things like "Colton for president."

So, these people have paid a total of about $570 to support their son/nephew/whomever. If we were all here only to be entertained, $30 would be a fair price for a night of entertainment. However, I'd bet that a solid majority of the audience is here tonight to support a loved one. If six or seven people show up to support each of the 28 fighters, we have an almost capacity crowd. These people are here because they're kind, supportive people—or people who know when they're more or less obligated to do something. They're not here primarily for entertainment. Which makes the whole $30 ticket price seem equivalent to charging $30 to watch a children's soccer game or piano recital or high school talent show. If your kid is participating in something, you're not allowed to say, "Sorry, I'd love to come, but $30 is a bit steep."

FIGHT NINE

Things people near me say during fight nine, in chronological order:

"Arf arf arf arf."

"That foot stomp was monstrous. Gave me a hard-on."

"Arf arf arf arf arf arf arf arf."

Toward the end of the fight a man in the audience in front of me starts combing his hair.

BILLY'S FIGHT

No one's been able to give me any advance information on Billy's opponent. Not that advance info would help. Whenever I ask an MMA fighter about someone's upcoming opponent, they use the phrase "pretty tough." As in "should be a pretty tough fight" or "I hear he's pretty tough." I suspect that there's some sort of MMA gentlemen's agreement that you never say that your friend's upcoming opponent sucks. Whether you win or lose, you look much better if your opponent is pretty tough. Or else maybe everyone who's ever had an amateur MMA fight really is pretty tough.

The announcer tells us that Billy's opponent, Joe, is from the Fort Lewis Army fight team. Fort Lewis is a sad, sad place just south of Tacoma on Interstate 5. Joe is short and mostly muscle and as he walks out he gives his coach a low, middle, and high five. Just above his left hip he has a tattoo that looks like a Rorschach test. He doesn't look nervous. I have no idea whether Joe's been in actual combat, but I imagine that being in a military conflict is one of the few experiences that makes MMA seem like a good way to unwind. Joe actually looks like he's pretty tough.

When the fight starts it immediately becomes clear that Joe is a natural athlete, and it's a pleasure to watch him fight. He's never out of position, never wastes any movement. He lacks the understandable franticness that marks even experienced fighters, and calmly kicks ass. It's almost disturbing how calm he is. This is, of course, unfortunate for Billy. In the third round, Joe catches Billy in a chokehold, which seems like a relatively merciful ending. Billy got his ass kicked, but his ass was kicked in such a thorough and efficient manner that, even if you like Billy, it was almost fun to watch.

FIGHT ELEVEN

This is labeled the light heavyweight championship. The people who organize these fights always put the championship fights last, as a climax to the evening. Shakespearian plot structure it isn't, but it does ensure that most people will stay until the end, thus purchasing more from the concession stands. A large part of the crowd is chanting, "Weezer. Weezer. Weezer." One of the fighters raps along with his song as he walks to the cage. Everyone stands for this fight. Shortly into the first round there's a takedown. I can't see anything. Too many yelling and screaming heads in the way. Something exciting is going on and I'm missing out. This is what I get for trying to sneak in. I hear the distinct sound of fat being slapped. A prepubescent male voice yells, "Come on, light his ass up!" The crowd gets louder and then the ref blows the whistle. Someone has won, but I don't know what happened. As I'm leaving everyone is talking about the fight and how great it was. The announcer says, "I've been doing this a long time, and you are the best goddamn crowd I've ever seen." I'm honored.

CHAPTER 9

THE RETURN OF CHAD

CHAD HAS FINALLY AGREED to take another fight, nearly nine months after his last non-tag-team match. We don't know anything about his opponent except that he's supposedly a champion in a local MMA league near Gig Harbor, about an hour and a half southwest of Seattle.

Chad's not actually defending his *Ax Fighting* belt tonight though, but is instead fighting for the *Peninsula* MMA *Throwdown* 145-pound title belt. If Chad wins the belt tonight and then returns home to north Seattle, it seems like this poor backwater MMA league will be forever without its 145-pound title belt unless it can send a champion up to find and then defeat Chad and return the belt to its rightful home. I'm assured that this isn't how it works but am not told how it actually does.

My opinion—which no one objects to—is that this fight doesn't matter for Chad's MMA career. So little is known about

Chad's opponent or this MMA scene out on the Peninsula that, if Chad loses, he can just make it seem like he lost to some backwoods beast who's on his way to the professional circuit. But if Chad beats this unknown opponent, it won't really improve his standing in the north-Seattle MMA scene, since he's already at the top of that pile, ready to take on any worthy challengers. So it seems like this fight is more of a training exercise than anything, preparing Chad for a yet-to-be-scheduled important fight in the future.

Tonight's event is called *The Peninsula MMA Throwdown Featuring DJ Charlee Brown*. It's at the Key Peninsula Civic Center in Vaughn, Washington, which isn't so much a town as a collection of vacant lots and houses with cars on blocks in their yards. The actual Civic Center is in a clearing in the woods. We park with two tires in a drainage ditch. A reader board informs us that we've just missed an event called "Scrapbooking."

The inside of the facility has a community theater stage, basketball hoops, and a fighting cage. The facility appears to be decorated for a high school prom. All the windows are covered by vinyl sheets decorated with stars and moons and city skylines at night, and across the stage are several strings of stars made from cardboard and glitter glue. The prom theme must have been "Starry Night" or "Romance Under the Stars." It smells like chewing tobacco.

I'm here with my mom (Terry) and dad (Steve), Brady, and Jake. Steve once broke his arm during a JV wrestling match in ninth grade, so he knows a thing or two about mixed martial arts and has positioned himself so he can speak his wisdom directly into my ear.

Our music tonight is provided by DJ Charlee Brown. DJ Charlee Brown is wearing an oversized yellow T-shirt with the recognizable black Charlie Brown squiggle across the front. It seems relevant to point out that DJ Charlee Brown has a different skin color from the original Charlie Brown. DJ Charlee Brown has two tables of complicated-looking equipment and always seems immensely busy. Yet throughout the night he only cues songs, which seems like something he could do with a standard MP3 player.

The announcer is dressed in a suit, but although he's at least 35 he still looks like he's wearing his father's suit. He's so nervous he's visibly shaking. He reads every word he says from three-by-five note cards. Every single word, including words like "hello" and "thank you for coming out tonight." He speaks in the same monotone as a fifth grader giving a class presentation on the pyramids. He welcomes all of us and describes DJ Charlee Brown as "very talented."

FIGHT ONE

Steve spends most of this fight giving me a thorough explanation of what a farmer's tan is. He describes it as "unsophisticated." The farmer's tan in question is worn by a fighter the crowd calls "Pit," who's representing Team Rude Awakening. Pit likes to throw illegal elbows.

Steve's take on fight one, "This is so boring."

Pit wins, but instead of a trophy he receives a goody bag. The losing fighter receives a goody bag of a different color. The contents of the goody bags are not revealed to the audience.

At the end of the fight the announcer says, "Tonight's event is brought to you by Smokin Hot Espresso. How hot can you handle it." Again, this is read from a note card in a monotone.

The woman sitting in front of me, who looks like she's in her early fifties, is reading a thick novel with not-very-small print. She didn't look up from her book during the first fight. This doesn't seem like an ideal reading environment. I lean over her shoulder enough to see that the novel's title is *Sizzling Sixteen*. She is on page 121.

FIGHT TWO

Chad and others involved with *Ax Fighting* claim that it's the most prestigious amateur fighting series in Western Washington. They claim that a lot of fighters have to work their way up the ranks before they even get a chance to fight at *Ax Fighting*, and that they're honored just to participate. I always assumed this was not true, since every *Ax Fighting* event has several fights between fighters who've never fought before. But the second fight at *Peninsula* MMA *Throwdown* makes me question my stance.

The first fighter to come out, Gabe, has a mohawk and a tank top tan. There are enough tank top tans on fighters tonight that from here on out they'll be left to your imagination. Gabe looks like he's 6 feet tall and 130 pounds. This is a 150-pound fight. Steve's take on Gabe, "He's going to get hurt."

Steve said this before he saw Gabe's opponent, Roger. Roger is about 5 feet 8 inches and 130 pounds, and that's not all muscle. Roger and Gabe both look like the sort of guys who were regularly locked inside dumpsters during high school. I'm betting they started fighting to get tough so they could one day confront their bullies and show them who's the Renaissance Faire pussy now.

And, oh, are these guys angry. They spend most of the fight throwing wild Go-Fuck-Your-Mother punches that don't connect. Roger tries kneeing Gabe in the chest. Gabe tries a backwards-spinning roundhouse kick aimed at Roger's head. It misses.

The problem is that both Roger and Gabe are incredibly weak. Their punches—when they actually land them—don't do anything. They aren't strong enough to knock each other out, so it goes to the judges, who have the depressing task of deciding which of these guys deserves to be called a winner. They decide it's Gabe. I can only imagine how this will affect Roger's anger level.

Steve's take, "The blonder your hair, the more fun you have."
Book Lady is on page 148 of *Sizzling Sixteen*.

FIGHT THREE

Most MMA coaches are surly, tattooed guys who look like they've at some point clubbed another person with a broken pool cue. The first fighter in this fight, James, is coached by his mother. My family members and I debate whether she's best described as "overweight" or "obese," but we all agree that either adjective should be preceded by "very." Instead of carrying the usual rags for cleaning up bodily fluids, she has an armful of blue bath towels.

James's opponent immediately punches James in the face 11 times. James's mother-coach has no visible reaction to the beating. DJ Charlee Brown cues the song "You Shook Me All Night Long."

FIGHT FOUR

We're now on page 162 of *Sizzling Sixteen*. I'm able to make out a single line of dialogue from the text, "I bet Chopper got money."

Tonight's ring girls are the staff of the above-mentioned Smokin Hot Espresso, which, from what I can tell, is a local drive-thru espresso stand where the baristas wear lingerie or swimsuits, a sort of hybrid of Starbucks and Sugars Night Club. I'm not sure about the Washington State health code's stance on near-naked people pulling espresso shots and steaming milk.

Between rounds, two of the Smokin Hot Espresso girls enter the ring. One holds the sign with the round number while the other throws a T-shirt into the crowd and tries to look sexy. Jake and I agree that our future happiness depends on obtaining one of these T-shirts. During fight four Jake accidentally kicks Book Lady while trying to retrieve a T-shirt. Book Lady says, "Thanks for kicking me." Brady tells Jake he's a little dick for disturbing her reading.

FIGHT FIVE

The first fighter has apparently ordered a novelty-sized cup to protect his testicles. I leave to find something to drink.

The only beverage sold at the concession stand outside is a drink called "TURN ON: A Love Drink." The can's label says, "WARNING: this beverage will AROUSE you!" A TURN ON flier at the table says "TURN ON in the Media!" above a picture of Donald Trump.

Brief research later reveals that TURN ON is not FDA-approved, but that's the least of my TURN ON concerns. Is this really the time and the place to get turned on? Do I want to appear as though mixed martial arts arouses me? And what sort of mess are we creating, cramming hundreds of people into a sweaty gym and then offering no hydration options except a TURN ON Love Drink? What good could possibly come from this?

I skip the TURN ON beverage booth.

FIGHT SIX
One guy grabs the other guy by the scruff of the neck and punches him five or six times in the upper lip.

FIGHT SEVEN
Between rounds when the ring girls are distributing T-shirts, the T-shirt thrower makes eye contact and throws one directly to me. She doesn't throw it quite far enough, but any reasonable observer would have to admit that the intent is there. I may be a bit too aggressive with the whole ordeal. Elbows are involved. Some chairs fall over. Everyone in the vicinity is looking at me like, *It's just a T-shirt*. I quickly give the shirt to Jake, sort of redeeming myself.

FIGHT EIGHT
This fight is a Muay Thai fight. One of the fighters is wearing jewels and beads and a tennis-racket-shaped headdress. That is, he's dressed like a witch doctor. Before the fight starts, he does a dance accompanied by what sounds like snake-charming music. He starts on his belly and dances his way to his feet. Once on his feet, he continues dancing in a way that looks like a mix of karate and belly dancing. The dance lasts more than two minutes.

He then gets the shit kicked out of him in 45 seconds. He's punched several times and is then donkey kicked in the cheekbone. He is unconscious. When the paramedics come into the ring one of them is laughing. The fighter ends up being okay.

Steve's take, "He can dance better than he can fight, that's for sure. I tell ya."

INTERMISSION

Jake returns from a snack run to report that a female beverage vendor has asked him if "he wanted to be turned on." He has also recently unfolded his T-shirt to discover that it's size adult XL and that the shirt's front features a screen-print of a woman wearing fishnet stockings and not much else.

Steve then returns from his own snack run with a tale from the TURN ON beverage table that I refuse to transcribe but involves the phrase "young ladies."

Brady and I, in our ongoing effort to raise our own self-esteem at Jake's expense, convince Jake that he should get his shirt signed by the Smokin Hot Espresso girls.

Jake asks our mom, "You won't get mad at me?"

Mom, "No."

Jake, "Will you give me money to do it?"

Jake leaves, and after he's gone for about eight minutes, Steve begins to worry. I assume he's worried about what's happening to Jake what with all these young ladies hopped up on TURN ON Love Drinks.

When Jake finally returns, he doesn't have his shirt autographed, but he does have a year-length pin-up calendar featuring the staff of Smokin Hot Espresso wearing lingerie. They don't exactly have their legs crossed. On their respective pages, the girls have written things like, "Stay sexy Jakie Poo xoxo."

Jake states, for the record, that he doesn't know how he feels about this.

FIGHT THIRTEEN

At the start of this fight, Book Lady sets down *Sizzling Sixteen*, stands up, and walks closer to the ring. At last check-in she was on page 257, for a total of 136 pages read tonight. Earlier we overheard her say that she's here to watch her son tonight. One can only assume how she feels about her son fighting at an event like this.

Her son's opponent looks like he was cut out of *Men's Fitness* magazine. He is 205 pounds of sweaty bodybuilder-style muscle, the kind of muscle built by doing bench press while looking in a mirror. He doesn't actually have a barbed-wire tattoo around his bicep, but it's there in spirit.

And then Book Lady's son, Mike, comes out. He looks like a normal 205-pound adult male who jogs three times a week and maybe plays some disc golf on weekends. He looks like it would never cross his mind to go tanning or to worry about the definition in his triceps.

Steve says, "I think this Mike guy is in trouble."

Book Lady has the same patient facial expression most people wear during the Pledge of Allegiance.

The fight begins, and Men's Fitness immediately manhandles Mike to the floor and starts punching him in the face, which is smashed into the cage not far from Mike's mom. For a moment Mike has a look of pain that I've never seen on someone over the age of five. He appears to look directly at his mom. Men's Fitness punches Mike in the back of the head for 15 seconds until the ref blows the whistle. No discernible emotion from Mike's mother.

When Mike—also expressionless in the exact same way as his mother—leaves the ring, Men's Fitness stays in the cage. He is handed the microphone. The crowd is quiet. Men's Fitness invites his girlfriend into the ring.

The girl looks exactly how I would've pictured Men's Fitness's romantic interest: bleached hair, tanning-booth tan, tight red tank top, tight torn jeans. She appears to be the only person in the room who hasn't discerned what's about to happen.

Then Men's Fitness—who, I suspect, shaved his chest pre-fight for maximum glisten—says, "Will you spend the rest of your life with me?" There is no discernible verbal answer from the girl, but they do some onstage groping. Some people applaud.

Brady's take, "They were fighting for her. The winner got her."

My take is that this is the most depressing moment in the history of amateur mixed martial arts. I strongly suspect this was a setup, that it was arranged for Men's Fitness to have an opponent he could easily knock out as a setup for his proposal. And that proposal, doesn't every girl dream of being proposed to after her sweaty boyfriend just kicked the crap out of someone? So, Book Lady sat through two hours of noise and violence, diligently reading her novel, thinking she was here to watch her son compete, and instead watched her son get humiliated for 46 seconds as a setup to the worst proposal man hath wrought. My objective journalistic stance is that Men's Fitness is a terrible human being.

CHAD'S FIGHT

Chad's opponent has a head shaved to the skull, tattoos, and a ring of facial hair around his mouth. My family says that the only fair way to describe him is that he wouldn't stick out at a white-supremacist function. When he and Chad are face-to-face before the fight, he gives Chad an I-will-eat-all-your-future-children stare.

I know that Chad's opponent probably wasn't responsible for what happened in the preceding fight, but at the very least he's from the same geographical area, and I can't help but think that there's a little bit of justice when Chad throws him to the ground, punches him a few times, and knocks him out in under two minutes. Chad doesn't get a trophy, and they've conveniently run out of goody bags. He does get another belt, though.

After the crowd leaves, the floor is littered with bottles of chewing tobacco spit.

CHAPTER 10

A FIGHT THAT NO ONE REALLY WANTED TO SEE

WITH A RECORD OF ten wins, a loss he avenged, and three title belts, Chad has accomplished everything one could hope to accomplish in the 145-pound weight class of the north Seattle suburbs amateur mixed martial arts circuit. If Chad were interested in giving us a satisfying sports story, he'd be taking a professional fight or at least a tough amateur fight. Instead, Chad is fighting someone named Mike.

Chad wasn't supposed to fight Mike, but Chad's previous opponent backed out earlier in the week because, according to Chad, "He saw my last fight." It's remarks like these that make me think it'd be terribly interesting to see Chad get knocked the fuck out.

But tonight doesn't look promising. Mike has fought only twice, and since Mike accepted this fight on two days' notice, he likely didn't have time to cut weight. There's really no way he can weigh more than 150 pounds at fight time, compared to Chad, who will have rehydrated to nearly 165 pounds. So Chad has a huge advantage over Mike in both experience and weight. No one's expecting this to be a competitive fight.

The big mystery that no one can really explain to me is why Chad has gone almost ten months without a fight where he wasn't the heavy favorite. Surely by now a somewhat worthy contender should have risen through the ranks or overcome any injuries to fight Chad. I'm not sure whether this hypothetical worthy contender just doesn't exist or whether Chad is for some reason not accepting a fight with him. I'm beginning to suspect it's the latter.

Whatever the reason, if I wanted to spend three hours and $30 to see Chad beat up someone he outweighed by 15 pounds, I'd take a taxi to our parents' house and watch home videos of the time when we were kids and invented a game called "Border Crossing." If I still had time to spare after that, I'd listen to my dad explain why we should kill all the bears, especially those living in national parks.

So, to once again avoid spending money, I've made myself a press pass. Brief Internet research has led me to believe that most press passes are printed on drugstore copy machines and laminated with Scotch tape, so I suspect that my press pass—designed in Photoshop, printed in color on glossy cardstock, with its own plastic sleeve, and an expiration date (because if it were a fake press pass, would I really have put an expiration date on it?)—might actually be too professional.

I am told that this won't work. I am told that the doormen at *Ax Fighting* events are ex-fighters trained to deal with just this sort of situation. "So what if your press pass has a lanyard," I'm told. When I actually get to the front of the show-your-ticket line, the ticket taker looks all of 17 and seems generally scared to be here. I hold up my pass, nod at him, walk right by, and pause to note all the non-press people who paid $30 to get in tonight.

I sit between Jake and Jake's next-door neighbor friend, who requests that in all written material I refer to him as "Bruce." Bruce spends most of the evening texting with Rachel. Before the fights begin, Bruce informs us that it would not hurt at all to get punched by someone wearing boxing gloves because, "they're, like, padded." Jake and I tell Bruce that there's an easy way to find out if he's right. Bruce declines because, "whatever."

The first two fighters have a combined total of zero wins and zero losses. The most interesting part of this fight is when the ring girl enters after the first round and appears to have forgotten to bring the sign that says "Round Two." So instead of a sign, she's holding up a single finger. The problem here is that she should be holding up two fingers, not one. In fact, ring girls don't ever announce round one, since it's usually obvious that the first round is the first round. They don't even have a sign that says "Round One." I'm not sure what sort of deductive logic this ring girl used to arrive at the round-one conclusion. Bruce states that Rachel is hotter than all the ring girls.

A SUMMARY OF FIGHTS TWO, THREE, SIX THROUGH EIGHT, TEN, TWELVE, AND FOURTEEN

The word "amateur" is used mostly in two ways: 1) amateur as in "unpaid," and 2) amateur as in "god-awful." Eight of the fights tonight are amateur in both senses. One fight deteriorates into a game of paddle fisties. One fighter turns his back on his opponent and runs away. One person throws a kick so weak that his opponent catches it in his hand, and then both fighters stand there awkwardly. One guy tries to choke his opponent by covering his opponent's mouth with his hand. Several fighters intentionally tangle themselves in the guard ropes. One fight ends up with guy one riding on guy two's back while guy two tries to buck guy one off. It's a disgrace to amateur mixed martial arts.

FIGHT FOUR

One of the fighters in this fight is a pudgy Hispanic named Jesus. He loses. People near me then make jokes based on the concept of Jesus Christ being a pudgy Hispanic that loses an amateur mixed martial arts fight.

FIGHT FIVE

I pay for a $2 slice of pizza with nickels.

FIGHT NINE

A man in the standing room section in front of us, wearing a "DEATH POWER" T-shirt, raps along to a song that includes the words "*strippers in body bags*." I realize that any attempt to find the title for this song will involve Googling "strippers in body bags."

QUOTES FROM AUDIENCE MEMBERS THAT AREN'T ANY MORE ACCEPTABLE EVEN WHEN TAKEN IN CONTEXT

"He has the biggest hard-on right now."

"Tea-bag him!"

"Let's raise the roof!"

FIGHT ELEVEN, WHICH SHOULD BE UNDERSTOOD IN THE CONTEXT OF ABOVE SECTION

Jake returns from the concession stand to report that a stranger has purchased him a Gatorade. Jake says, "This is a good place to make friends."

NANNA AND BOPPA

At some point during the night my Catholic grandparents—who will be called Nanna and Boppa—arrive, yet they spend about an hour in the foyer because it's "too loud" in the gymnasium proper. I'm not sure who thought they'd have a pleasant evening at an event called *Ax Fighting 30*. These are the same grandparents who declared Christmas "ruined" four years ago when a still-unidentified party put a box of Magnum XL Condoms in the family gift exchange.

Nanna and Boppa enter the gymnasium proper just in time to catch a fight between two girls who haven't fought before. One of them, Regan, sporting the same haircut as Bruce, has a pre-fight posse-train of 23 people. Regan quickly chokes out the other girl with what someone calls a "flop choke."

Dad, "Is that a guy fighting a girl?"

Nanna, "Is that a girl?"

Boppa, "What'd she do to win that?"

CHAD'S FIGHT

Chad enters the ring by leaping over the rails, instead of sliding through them like a normal fighter, i.e., someone who doesn't deserve a thorough beating.

Steve says, "Chip off the ol' block."

Chad gets a quick takedown and starts punching. I've seen this before. Nanna puts her hands over her mouth. She rocks in her chair. Mike is bleeding from his face. Chad and Mike look like they've been splashing around in a puddle of Mike's blood. The ref pauses the fight to clean up. Boppa is watching with the same expression he has when he's watching televised golf. He served in Korea.

Mom asks, "Do they do HIV testing?" They don't. They don't do blood testing of any sort at the amateur level, which is terrifying in a way I fortunately don't have time to dwell on.

The fight resumes. Mike's mouthguard falls out. It's not cleaned before he puts it back in. This is the least of his worries. In round three, Chad has finally beaten Mike enough for the ref to end the fight. I'm doing my best to imagine what could've made this beating worth it for Mike—or why Chad would want to be involved in something like that—and I'm coming up blank.

CHAPTER 11

LOSING A BELT IN THE MOST HUMILIATING WAY POSSIBLE

THE VIABLE CONTENDER CHAD has been waiting for has finally arrived. His name is Drew Brokenshire, and he has a record of fourteen wins and four losses. Drew has been out with an injury for months, but now he's back and has challenged Chad for his belt. Chad, however, has declined Drew's challenge, and according to the rules of amateur MMA, if you decline a challenge, you must forfeit your belt. It's similar to the rules for duels in 19th-century Russian novels.

Chad didn't give up his belt because he turned to professional fighting. Far from it. Chad turned down Drew's challenge because he's been working out of state on test flights for the Boeing 787 and hasn't been able to train consistently. I've been unable to gauge exactly how Chad feels about forfeiting his belt, but I'm sure he's aware that saying, "I'd fight you, but I have to work," is exactly what a total pussy would say.

So instead Drew is fighting Kale Bradford, a 145-pound fighter who trains at Charlie's Combat Club. Journalistic responsibility seems to require that I attend *Ax Fighting 33* to witness the fight for the belt that was formerly my brother's. There's a chance that if Chad's work schedule cooperates and he stops being a puss he'll fight the winner of this fight to regain his dignity and delay his move to the pro ranks, where I'll all but guarantee a beating or two awaits him.

I'm accompanied tonight by Chad, several of his friends, and my beautiful wife, who has agreed to attend and provide color commentary for *Ax Fighting 33* under the condition that in all written material I refer to her as My Beautiful Wife (henceforth MBW).

We arrive at Edmonds Community College right as the fights start. The $30 bleacher seating has already sold out, and all that remains are $35 seats in the folding chairs closer to the ring. I've brought my homemade press pass for just this purpose, but while we're in line Chad appears with two reserved-seating tickets for MBW and me, rendering my press pass unnecessary.

AN ANTHROPOLOGICAL ANALYSIS OF TONIGHT'S AUDIENCE

I have no way to confirm this, but we have to be setting a per-capita record for Nickelback fans.

I've now attended enough amateur MMA fights in the Seattle suburbs to notice that the audience at these things is largely composed of a certain Pacific Northwest subculture—a subculture that might be foreign to anyone who hasn't spent much time in the area. What I'm describing here is, really, a male subculture. It seems fair to say that most of the females at these events are here because of guys, one way or another. The unifying factor for this subculture is hard to pin down—it isn't economics or class or even race, really. I've lived among these people most of my life, and though I probably don't qualify as one of them, I've observed a few common characteristics:

- The worst insult you can throw around is "pussy." Close behind is probably any number of variations on "homosexual."

- People tend to drink Miller Light or Bud Light or a beverage known as "Pink Panty Droppers."

- Most in this demographic probably have at least one close friend or family member in the Boeing Machinists Union.

- Sometimes they'll play a yard game of unknown origin called "Arizona Horseshoes."

- Sleeveless shirts and arm tattoos and black T-shirts are totally acceptable wardrobe options for any type of event or outing.

- People here don't tend to follow traditional team sports. Perhaps this is obvious. If they follow a sport at all it's the NFL, and then they're guaranteed diehard Seahawks fans.

Beyond these characteristics, this subculture is tough to pin down. I have no idea what sort of political views they hold. If you're not familiar with this group, it might be tempting to label them "white trash." But they're not, not really at all. Quite a few of them—probably more than half— have gone to college, and most of them value hard work and making money. Community is important to them, and they value having a good time, whatever that might mean.

In short, this subculture is the perfect audience for mixed martial arts, even though it existed well before mixed martial arts even had a name. Specifically, it's the perfect audience for amateur mixed martial arts. They love watching individual sports like wrestling, and they love it even more when they know the athletes—and they don't mind the violence. It seems unlikely that someone created and marketed amateur MMA just to fill this consumer niche. In Charlie's case, he started training fighters and holding events simply because that's what he enjoyed doing and knew how to do, and it was just good luck that an audience for MMA already existed.

There's something else going on with the audience at amateur MMA events, something positive. Now that word has spread about Chad's fighting career, his fights have turned into community reunions. Old friends from high school come out, people we worked with at the local swimming pool, our parents' neighbors, and people I know we know even though I can never remember how we know them. Those people. In a way, amateur MMA events serve the same role among our community that little league baseball did 15 years ago or that high school football games did 10 years ago.

This is one part of being an amateur MMA fan that I can feel good about. If you ignore the violence, what's left resembles a local, community thing, like a farmer's market or a garage sale or a neighborhood Easter egg hunt. It's people from our community supporting other people in our community doing something they enjoy. Sometimes fans or promoters of professional sports talk about how supporting your local team is a way to strengthen the community and support the local economy—you usually hear more of this when a team's owners are trying to convince the government to subsidize a stadium. This sort of talk has always struck me as hollow. It's unlikely that I'll see anyone I know at a pro sporting event, the athletes on pro sports teams aren't usually homegrown, and the owners don't always even live in the same state or country. But with amateur MMA, it's different. Our whole section of the bleachers is occupied by people I grew up with. All the athletes are local—I know quite a few of them personally, and I'm familiar with quite a few more from high school wrestling. And for all my complaining about and avoidance of the ticket prices, the money is ultimately going to a local entrepreneur—Charlie—who basically built the whole north-Seattle amateur MMA scene from scratch over a couple of decades. He deserves the proceeds from people who haven't figured out creative ways around the ticket price.

FIGHT ONE

This fight is between a Mexican man and an African American man. Chad and his friend Robert offer racially-charged commentary for the whole fight. This commentary is not written down, despite Chad's completely valid objection, "Like we need to be politically correct here."

MBW's analysis, "The black guy looks a lot stronger. Just in terms of muscles."

FIGHT THREE

The two men sitting to my left are on an iPhone looking at an x-ray of a human spine. They are discussing vertebrae. They are not watching the fight. They soon leave.

The fight itself is a 215-pound kickboxing match. It features a moment where a chubby guy is kneed straight in his enormous belly. His belly simply swallows the knee. The knee disappears for a moment before the belly spits it back out.

FIGHT FOUR

The fighter in the blue corner enters the ring accompanied by a song that keeps rhyming "*fuck*" with "*fuck*" and other conjugations of "*fuck*."

MBW's take on this fighter, "He looks like he's been in jail or something. Looks like a serial killer."

It's true. He has an orange mohawk, a goatee you could hide a shiv in, and what can only be described as methamphetamine eyes. He's not big or even muscular, but I'm receiving reports from further down the row that he looks like the pedophile from the TV show *Prison Break*, which I haven't seen and now will not see.

The only note I have about the second fighter is that his posse is the goofiest looking bunch of misfits in the history of MMA.

In the first round Meth Eyes gets his ass almost literally handed to him. At one point his opponent has him bent in such a way that his ass is just inches from his mouth.

This angers Meth Eyes. At the start of the second round he runs at his opponent and throws a huge no-one-hands-my-ass-to-me punch. His opponent, in a move that's both smart and awesome, simply ducks and tosses Meth Eyes to his back.

Someone behind me is yelling, "Crucifix! Crucifix!"

In MMA, there are at least two ways to handle being on your back. The first way is to wrap up your opponent's arms and legs and hunt for ways to choke or harm him. This is called "guard," and it makes for a more or less neutral position. The second way, which we're going to call the "Meth Eyes Approach," is to flop on your back, go limp, and just give up, letting your opponent pummel your face until the ref stops the fight.

Meth Eyes goes to his corner and stands there, pissed that he lost, his face flush and smeared with blood. This doesn't make him look any less like a serial killer. For the rest of the night he lurks in the area behind our chairs, stretching and pacing.

FIGHT FIVE

On a trip to the restroom, I see a cluster of tall white men in community college basketball uniforms. They're peering into the gym, looking confused. It seems they came to shoot some hoops, only to find that the gym was being used for decidedly non-hoop-shooting purposes.

FIGHT SIX

Someone behind me keeps yelling, "Push on his face!" Not an actual MMA move.

MBW'S COMMENTARY ON THE RING GIRLS, COLLECTED THROUGHOUT THE NIGHT

MBW's analysis of the ring girls in general, "The ring girls are so disgusting."

MBW's stance on the ring girls' attire, "When you really think about it, the idea that they wear bathing suits is just sickening. I mean, they could just wear really skanky clothes. It's not subtle at all."

MBW's assessment of the ring girl in the pink bathing suit, "The one in the pink bathing suit doesn't even have big boobs."

MBW's assessment of the ring girl in the red bathing suit, "She's awfully short. Those boobs don't look real either. I'm sorry, but they don't."

MBW's continued assessment of the ring girl in the red bathing suit, "Looks like a porn star. That hair."

MBW's take on the ring girl in the black bathing suit, "She's got more cellulite than I'd like people to see. I'm just being bitchy though."

FIGHT SEVEN: GIRL VERSUS GIRL, PART ONE

This is the first of three female-versus-female fights tonight. The fighter in the blue corner is named Ashley. She looks like what my dad would call a very nice young lady. She has pale skin, strawberry blonde hair tied into a ponytail, and looks like a perfectly healthy 140-pound female. Or, as Chad puts it, she looks like she would "take fourth place in a wet T-shirt contest." Her opponent, Jamie Gonzales, who trains at Charlie's Combat Club, is 140 pounds of fem-muscle and, as MBW says, "has a very nice tan. She's very toned. Or maybe she might be Mexican."

What follows is the night's real downer. Jamie shoves Ashley to the mat, straddles her, and punches her again and again in the baby-fat face. Ashley takes her beating quietly, without much of a struggle, just the way you'd expect a very nice young lady to take such a beating.

It's sad, seeing a nice person get beat up like this. What makes it worse is that there's really no one to blame. Ashley can't be blamed for signing up. She probably somehow thought she had a chance. And Jamie's not really at fault for doing exactly what she was supposed to do, that is, win. The people who arrange the fights can't really be blamed either, since they arrange the fights according to fighters' records and don't have anything to gain from mismatches. It seems that we just live in a universe where, in the midst of an otherwise enjoyable and entertaining evening of athletic competition and mild violence, a very nice young girl can get her face beaten into a bloody mess.

MBW's take, "If I won, I wouldn't want to take a photo with a ring girl."

FIGHT EIGHT

The second fighter's intro song is evidently not a song at all but one of those spoken interludes sometimes found between tracks on rap albums. I only have the time and the emotional wherewithal to write down the first sentence, which was a sort of thesis statement for the next 45 seconds of audio, "I will tie you to a fucking bedpost with your ass cheeks spread out."

A small girl holding a stuffed pink unicorn soon sits in the vacant seat to my left.

MBW is now playing games on her smart phone. She states for the record that she is sort of bored.

FIGHT NINE

This one's a boxing match between someone named David and someone the announcer calls Tim "One Punch" Abell. I suspect One Punch gave himself this nickname. It takes him significantly more than one punch to win the fight.

FIGHT TEN: GIRL VERSUS GIRL, PART TWO

The announcer seems uncertain whether we're ready for another women's MMA fight. We assure him that we are indeed ready for another women's MMA fight.

This one's in the 155-pound weight class or, as MBW says, the "that's a big girl" weight class. Everyone in our row agrees that we wouldn't have given it a second thought if the girl in the blue corner had been introduced as a guy.

MBW is unable to shed any feminine light on why girls seem unable to block punches.

FIGHT ELEVEN

At one point in the first round, the gym is almost totally silent with boredom.

INTERMISSION

A clothing company called Hooligan Inc. has a booth and a large banner in the southeast corner of the room. The banner says "Hooligan" and then, in a slightly smaller font, it says, "myspace.com/hooligan_inc@yahoo.com."

This appears to be both a URL and an email address.

Elsewhere in the gym is the sound booth, staffed by two young males around age 12. They are wearing T-shirts that say "TapouT." One is cradling a basketball. In a brief interview, they confirm that they are responsible for tonight's volume levels and music selection, except of course for fighters' intro songs, which the fighters choose for themselves. They then make it clear that they are not interested in further journalistic inquiries.

Two of the ring girls spend the intermission furiously texting. The third chews gum and gazes at the ring.

MBW's take on the intermission, "I'm bored."

At the end of the intermission a man in a suit steps into the ring with the microphone. He tells us he's a representative of *Northwest FightScene*, nwfightscene.com, which has recently issued some sort of awards. One of these awards is "Best Amateur Promotion," which our very own *Ax Fighting* has won.

The award is given to Charlie and Eric, another local coach who helps run *Ax Fighting*. Charlie accepts the award with the stoic dignity of someone who's tolerating something he's getting paid to tolerate. I'm told that there are photos floating around of Eric and Charlie standing in a room plastered with $20 bills brought in through *Ax Fighting*.

FIGHT TWELVE

MBW's phone has died, so she's now on her work phone playing a primitive game of *Where's Waldo?*

This fight is ended by a knockout punch. One of the fighters lands a fist right on his opponent's chin that produces a loud *clink* noise. It's either the sound of knuckle hitting jawbone or of teeth snapping shut or, most likely, both.

THE ZIPFIZZ GIRLS

This is the Zipfizz girls' third trip out to the ring to distribute Zipfizz, which now features the tagline "Healthy Energy Drink." I'm not positive on the technical distinction here, but one of the Zipfizz girls is short enough to qualify as a dwarf or a midget. Despite her height, her breasts appear large enough to topple even a normal adult human female. It's not exactly clear how she's staying upright.

There are five or six people in the audience standing and screaming for the Zipfizz girls to throw them canisters of Zipfizz and/or Zipfizz T-shirts. All of these people are white males over age 40. Typically the Zipfizz girls throw out canisters of Zipfizz one at a time, but these Zipfizz girls seem to have misunderstood their instructions and instead throw the entire plastic bag of Zipfizz canisters at once, to what must be one ecstatic middle-aged man.

FIGHT FOURTEEN

MBW has found Waldo.

FIGHT FIFTEEN: GIRL VERSUS GIRL, PART THREE

Someone has triggered the emergency exit alarm. The announcer says, "Someone has a loud-ass Motorola." This is met by one or two laughs, so he amends his joke to "loud-ass pacemaker," which is met by silence and more beeping.

Once the beeping stops, the announcer assures us that whatever the outcome of this next fight, we in the audience are the winners. This fight, he tells us, is for the 125-pound women's *Ax Fighting* MMA title.

The first girl, Amy, has a large and distinctly ellipsoid belly button. The other girl, Regan—whom we've seen fight before—has short hair and 19 people in her posse. The female fighters seem to have the largest posses. Someone in our row points out that, in case we hadn't noticed, Regan and Amy are oriented differently in a sexual way.

The first round confirms what you'd probably guess about 125-pound females: they can punch a lot, and they can punch accurately, but they just can't punch that hard.

In between rounds, the sound guys play filler music. For previous fights they've played Eminem or other 12-year-old-supported rap. For this fight—a fight that touches on some interesting questions regarding gender, especially gender as it relates to athletics—they play the chorus of that "My Humps" song.

In round three, someone behind me is yelling what sounds like "three way." At one point Regan punches Amy's blood-covered face and blood sprays into the first four rows. Regan wins. She's now the 125-pound women's *Ax Fighting* champion.

FIGHT SIXTEEN: THE 145-POUND TITLE FIGHT

Before the fight starts, the announcer asks several times if Chad Douglas is in the house. Chad finally enters the ring, carrying his *Ax Fighting* 145-pound title belt. The announcer introduces Chad as the current 145-pound *Ax Fighting* champion, and then asks him why he's not defending his title tonight.

"Taking a little intermission," Chad says. "Be back soon."

Showing an investigative tenacity that puts my interview with the 12-year-old sound guys to shame, the announcer asks Chad what's going on, what he's doing, what he's planning on doing, why he's not fighting. The (just barely) unspoken question, *Are you just being a pussy or what?*

Chad says, "A little intermission, and then we'll see what's up."

The whole thing seems aimed to humiliate Chad. It's mercifully ended for the actual fight to start.

The fighters are introduced as Drew "The Eternal Fire" Brokenshire and Kale (pronounced "collie") "Hawaiian Punch" Bradford. It's unclear whether these are established nicknames or ones that the announcer penned himself.

In the first round, Hawaiian Punch takes The Eternal Fire down and punches him a few times. It's hard to gauge this sort of thing, but it seems like both fighters are much tougher than anyone Chad has fought in recent history. While Hawaiian Punch continues the barrage, The Eternal Fire wraps his legs around Hawaiian Punch's head and grabs his arm. Hawaiian Punch stops punching and starts thrashing around, trying to dislodge The Eternal Fire. I still don't understand the geometry or physics of this move, but The Eternal Fire succeeds in bending Hawaiian Punch's arm in such a way so that Hawaiian Punch has two options: 1) let his elbow break and lose the fight, or 2) tap out and lose the fight. He chooses option two.

After The Eternal Fire is declared the winner, Chad then has to actually hand him the belt. Again, humiliating.

The lights go on. The ring girls are putting jeans on over their swimsuits. The emergency exit starts beeping again. If Chad fights another amateur fight, it will most likely be against Drew "The Eternal Fire" Brokenshire.

CHAPTER 12

BILLY'S FIRST TITLE FIGHT

TONIGHT I'M AT SHORELINE Community College in Shoreline, Washington, to watch Billy Walker fight "Krazy" Kris "The Crippler" Zorrer for the *Genesis Fights* bantamweight (135 pounds) mixed martial arts title. Since Billy's loss at *Knockout at the Nile 4*, he's come back and improved his record to seven and three, which is good enough for Billy to now fight for titles.

Tonight, Drew "The Eternal Fire" Brokenshire is also fighting, in a Muay Thai fight. Every once in a while MMA fighters will do a Muay Thai or kickboxing fight as a way of honing their skills with less pressure—because if an MMA fighter loses at Muay Thai, they always have the excuse that it isn't really what they train to do anyway.

But I suspect that Drew is taking this fight as a warmup for his all-but-guaranteed fight with Chad. Chad hasn't officially committed to fighting Drew, but he's strongly hinted that it's going to happen. Really, if Chad ever wants to fight again, he has to fight Drew. There's no way around it without it being totally obvious that Chad is avoiding a fight with Drew. So it seems almost inevitable that Chad and Drew will soon fight.

The official name of tonight's event is *Genesis Fights: Eclipse*. The graphics on the program are remarkably similar to the graphics of the popular young-adult paranormal-romance novel of the same *Eclipse* name. At no point tonight does it become clear what conclusions *Genesis Fights* management wants us to draw from this allusion.

This is my first time at a *Genesis Fights* event, and I don't know any of the staff. Nor do I know how to sneak into the gymnasium. So before I'm admitted into the gym proper, I'm forced to participate in a 22-minute drama regarding my press credentials. Not once does anyone from *Genesis Fights* staff give my homemade press pass more than a glance. If they had, they would've noticed that the expiration date had been amended with Wite-Out, and this whole ordeal would've been mercifully curtailed.

Young woman at the door, after glancing at my pass, "Oh okay. No problem. Just go talk to the people over there at the ticket counter."

Young man at the ticket counter, after a long pause, "I have to talk to someone."

Young woman who comes out to talk to me after I stand in the lobby for seven minutes writing mordant notes about *Genesis Fights* and its treatment of the press, "What publication are you with? McSweeney's? I've never heard of it. Well you see what happened is that you weren't already on the list and so what this means is that we don't actually have a seat saved for you."

Same passive-aggressive young woman after it's pointed out to her that the seating in the gymnasium is approximately half-full and that if worse comes to worst the press can stand on its own two feet, "Well okay, we didn't know about you ahead of time and you see we actually already have our own press here. You're going to have to pay for a ticket. Twenty-five dollars."

Same young woman after she's told that it "reflects quite poorly" on their organization to charge the press for entry and that the massive readership of this publication will surely read all sorts of negative things about *Genesis Fights*, "I'll go talk to someone."

Tough-looking management figure who comes out eight minutes later and who could easily kick my ass in a back room, "What publication did you say you were with?"

Second tough-looking management figure who comes out four minutes later with a smart phone and pulls up the publication in question and who also could easily kick my ass in a back room, maybe in some sort of good-cop bad-cop routine with the first guy, "I think I've seen this before."

First tough-looking management figure who returns a few minutes later and actually seems like a pretty decent guy, "Okay, you're in."

I promise to write nice things about *Genesis Fights*.

So let me say this, *Genesis Fights* might not be as racist as they first appear.

Each of the first four fights features an African American man fighting a Caucasian man. It seems improbable that this happened by chance. In a lull later in the evening, I calculate the odds of this happening by chance, using math I learned from televised poker. According to my math—which, I've been told, isn't correct in any way and assumes a number of parameters that can't accurately be assumed—if you start with four African Americans and four Caucasians, the odds of ending up with four interracial fights are just under 25 percent, far from impossible but still suspicious.

If you're interested, Caucasians win three out of the four fights. This sample is too small to draw any helpful statistical conclusions.

I'm standing at the edge of the gym, next to Chad, who's giving me the rundown on the fights tonight and the rundown on the blonde ring girl, "She needs to spend less time in the tanning booth and more time in the gym. And you can quote me on that."

About ten feet from us a young male is waiting in line for popcorn. He's wearing a T-shirt that reads "Shakespeare's Insults." This T-shirt contains a list of insults from Shakespeare's plays, e.g., "a fusty nut with no kernel" or "canker blossom." This young man's skin is vampire-white and he has a mullet so long it must've taken him the better part of his life to grow. He vanishes before I can ask him what exactly brought him to *Genesis Fights: Eclipse*.

FIGHT FIVE

Finally we have a same-race fight, Caucasian versus Caucasian. At one point in the first round, one fighter, lying on his back, bends his legs up and wraps them around the head-neck area of his opponent, who is sitting on top of him. They roll around and end in a position best described as "reverse cowboy."

In round two, there's a break in the fight for an unintentional nut kick. Never gets old. The fight later ends when one of the fighters won't stop bleeding. The winner is announced, and I'm not sure whether it's the bleeder or the guy who pulled the reverse-cowboy maneuver. Keeping track of fighters was much easier when it was color-coded.

FIGHT SIX

I'm now sitting in the bleachers on the west side of the gym, near a group of nine or so guys and two of their female companions. From what I can tell, they're a group of friends who still live in their hometown a few years after high school.

This fight is in what's called "A-Class" MMA. The only discernible difference between A-Class MMA and regular MMA is that A-Class fighters wear what are either shin pads or long socks.

The first fighter has a blue mohawk and bounces around like he's hopped up on Zipfizz. He tries five roundhouse kicks, and they all miss. On the sixth one his opponent grabs his foot. They end up lying on the mat, legs tangled in a Kama-Sutraish way. Blue Mohawk then starts punching his opponent in the back of the head until the ref stops him.

STATED NICKNAMES FOR TONIGHT'S FIGHTERS AND OTHER PRESENTERS, IN ALPHABETICAL ORDER

Black
Black Seminole, the
Crippler, the
Eternal Fire, the
Future, the
Johnny Boy

Jones, Darrick Bob
Krazy
Machine, the
Mankill
Nerd Rage
Ong Black
Pretty
Samurai, the
Showtime
Silent Assassin, the
Super Mario
Wizard, the

FIGHT SEVEN

The guys behind me accompany this fight with sound effects from the *Mortal Kombat* video game, like, "Fatality!" One of them sings two unprovoked verses of the Backstreet Boys song "I Want It That Way."

By round three, both fighters are so exhausted that they can't even throw punches, even though both are wide open for all sorts of punishment. Everyone else in the audience must be thinking exactly what I'm thinking, *I could dominate both of these pussies*.

One of the girls behind me has dropped her purse through the gaps between the bleachers. None of the guys will retrieve it for her.

INTERMISSION

The announcer is wearing a suit and tie, and it appears that he brushed his hair before tying it into a ponytail. It turns out that he also moonlights as a beatboxer. For the first 90 seconds of intermission he gives us a free sample of his beatboxing. It is surely the most professional beatboxing I've ever heard. He tells us his name is Darrick Bob Jones.

As I'm walking around the room I see someone with an actual Genesis-issued press pass. He is not taking notes. He doesn't even have note-taking equipment. Nor does he have a camera. Nor a tape recorder. In fact, while I spend the intermission industriously taking notes and trying to remember the AP-approved usage of "beatbox," this man, who holds a legitimate press pass and has a complimentary press seat just feet from the ring, spends the intermission dancing, in a half-assed way.

Our attention is then called to the ring for the announcement of the winner of the Xbox Kinect drawing. Mary Krab (correct spelling unknown) wins the Xbox Kinect. She is roughly mom-age and appears to be the person in the room least likely to use an Xbox Kinect.

FIGHT NINE: TAG-TEAM SUBMISSION

After Chad and Buck's tag-team submission fight last year, the video was posted on an MMA website, and in the comment section beneath it were dozens of remarks about how the whole thing and everyone involved were incredibly homosexual.

This fight is the same style as that fight, and I doubt that it would clear up anyone's questions about the sexual orientation of the whole affair.

Guy behind me, "I'm really confused right now."

FIGHT TEN

This fight is between two African American men, listed on the program as Naalij "The Black Seminole" Redicks and Taureen "Black" Washington.

One of the guys behind me is regaling his friends with a story that involved him (the narrator), "fucking chasing some guys down"—"by him-fucking-self"—and "fucking throwing them into the street."

This anecdote ends when one of the storyteller's friends declares, "It's punch time."

FIGHT ELEVEN: BILLY'S FIGHT

Full disclosure: Billy finds me twice tonight to tell me that "you better write something good about me this time." As an MMA fighter, Billy is capable of doing terrible things to me, so consider my journalistic integrity compromised. I intend to write nice things about Billy.

Billy's opponent, "Krazy" Kris "The Crippler" Zorrer, enters the ring to Tom Petty's "I Won't Back Down." Billy, whose beard isn't remotely pubic-looking, enters the ring to a song one of the guys behind me calls, "Oh shit. This is my jam."

Before the fight there's a ceremony where each of the fighters is allowed to look at the title belt but not touch it.

In the first round, the Krazy Crippler throws a huge punch that lands on Billy's jaw. Billy goes down. He later reports that for a few seconds he was out cold. He gets back up and nothing much happens the rest of the round.

The Crippler clearly won this round, so Billy—whose spandex shorts fit him nicely—needs to win both remaining rounds or knock out the Krazy Crippler.

In the second round, Billy kicks the Crippler a lot. The guys behind me are discussing a Major League Baseball "ruptured nut" incident. Billy likely won this round. Chad's girlfriend states that she will never again look at Billy the same with regards to the spandex shorts he's wearing.

At one point in the third round, Billy kicks the Crippler in the shin hard enough to knock him down. After he gets back to his feet, the Crippler flops on his back in a failed attempt to do some sort of leg bar thing to Billy. The round soon ends. A ring girl starts bringing out a "Round 4" sign but is waved away, this being a three-round fight. There's a Billy chant on the other side of the gym. Then it's announced, "By unanimous decision, the winner of this fight and the new *Genesis Fights* Bantamweight Champion is Billy Walker."

FIGHT TWELVE: THE FLYWEIGHT CHAMPIONSHIP

The first fighter's name is Luis Contreras. By way of Spanish pronunciation, the announcer uses English pronunciation while clearing his throat.

One of the guys behind me has been "waiting for this guy [Luis] to get his ass beat." And get his ass beat he does. His opponent picks him up by the legs and drops him, lands some good punches, and does a move that one of the guys behind me describes as a "toot 'n' bootie."

This ass beating continues into the second round until Luis, while getting his ass beat, somehow bends his opponent's elbow at an obtuse angle against the joint, and that's how Luis wins the fight.

FIGHT THIRTEEN

This is The Eternal Fire's Muay Thai fight, and I thought it would be great to get a scouting report on Drew to give a bit of a preview of what Chad's fight might look like, but I largely neglect to watch the fight because I'm listening to and transcribing a conversation among the guys behind me:

Guy one, "What's the plan after this?"

Guy two, "Getting drunk. What we always do."

Guy one, "That's what we always do."

Guy three, "The same thing we do every night, Pinky. Try to take over the world."

Drew ends up losing by decision. But, since this is a Muay Thai fight, it won't affect his mixed martial arts career at all, and he'll still fight Chad, as called for by the rules of amateur MMA title belts.

After the fight there's an altercation among the guys behind me. One of the guys says, "I do not want to play your guys' games anymore," and then he gets up and sits next to a sympathetic female. He tells her that his ears were "fucking flicked. Twice." And he's "fucking sick of it."

FIGHT FOURTEEN: HEAVYWEIGHT MMA TITLE

You can tell that the announcer has spent many a night looking in the mirror saying, "This is the main event." This is the main event, a fight for the *Genesis Fights* heavyweight title.

The first fighter enters the ring to the song "White and Nerdy" by Weird Al Yankovic. This fighter, whose stated nickname is "Nerd Rage," is probably 160 pounds of solid muscle and 65 pounds of solid fat.

The second fighter comes out to the song "Monster Mash" by Bobby (Boris) Pickett and The Crypt-Kickers. This fighter's stated nickname is "Mankill," and he's introduced as the "current undefeated Genesis heavyweight champion." He looks like a younger, angrier, dirtier Mr. Clean. Each of his pectoral muscles is roughly the size of my entire torso.

Judging by appearances, this is the biggest mismatch I've yet witnessed at an MMA fight. Chad tells me that Mankill's previous opponent backed out at the last minute, and Nerd Rage, who surely hadn't yet seen a picture of Mankill, accepted the fight.

If we can disregard the physical pain at stake here, it seems that Mankill is the one to pity. If he wins, so what—he beat a fat kid. If he loses, he lost to a guy with saggy nipples and a fantastic muffin top.

When the fight starts, to everyone's surprise Nerd Rage doesn't immediately receive a severe beating. Nerd Rage, it turns out, is a one-trick stallion. His trick is that he lowers his head, sprints at Mankill, and tackles him in the legs. And it works. At least four times he takes Mankill down with this run-at-him-really-fast-and-tackle-him move. When he connects, the ring shakes in a way that makes me question the integrity of its construction. Twice he almost shoves Mankill out of the ring onto the hardwood. The crowd loves it.

But in no way is Nerd Rage actually winning the fight. In the time Nerd Rage hasn't been tackling Mankill, Mankill has been punching Nerd Rage in the head, kicking him in the stomach, and generally manhandling him.

In round three, Nerd Rage knees Mankill in the face. It's exciting and, in amateur MMA, entirely illegal. He gets docked a point for it. I still haven't mastered the MMA scoring system, but I know that this is about as severe as getting docked a goal in soccer. Nerd Rage has almost no chance of actually winning.

As soon as the fight ends, they start playing the song "We Are the Champions." It's an interesting choice since MMA is an individual sport and thus "we" can never actually be the champions. It's announced that Mankill wins by unanimous decision. The only possible meaning that this song can have is that at *Genesis Fights: Eclipse* we are all the champions. Nerd Rage and Mankill hug each other.

CHAPTER 13

INTRODUCING JONNY GILBERTSON

TONIGHT I'M IN MY hometown of Everett, Washington, for a mixed martial arts event called *Chaos at the College*. The college here is Everett Community College, where right now a group of guys in the parking lot are smoking cigarettes and drinking beer near the open trunk of a small car. Tailgating, it seems.

I'm here to watch Jonny "Cage" Gilbertson fight for the CageWars number-one contender spot at 155 pounds. Jonny is good friends with Brady, and he grew up just down the street from us. Jonny is almost the quintessential example of the sort of fighter who a few decades ago would've gone on to wrestle at a top-notch college program but now instead turned to mixed martial arts. He grew up doing freestyle wrestling, and in high school wrestling he placed at the state tournament every year. He might hold the dubious title of being the best wrestler in Washington State to never actually win a high school state title. One time at a wrestling tournament, Jonny and I shared a room at the Night Lite Inn in Fife, Washington, where the carpet was inexplicably wet and left black stains on our socks.

Jonny fought three times while he was in college, usually in the fall when he had all summer to train. In these fights it was abundantly clear that Jonny was still largely a wrestler. He relied on his takedowns, on his mat work, rather than on any sort of stand-up boxing. Yet his wrestling skills were good enough to carry him, and he won all three of those fights. He graduated from Central Washington University in the spring and moved back to Western Washington, and now he seems intent on really pursuing his amateur MMA career.

Jonny's career is relevant to Chad's in a couple of ways. First, Jonny trains at Charlie's Combat Club, which gives Chad another solid opponent to train with. Second, and much more interesting, is that after this fight Jonny may very well drop to the 145-pound weight class. If this happened, it might force Chad to start taking professional MMA fights. It's a rigid code of honor in the MMA world—even at the professional level—that fighters from the same gym don't fight each other. But if Jonny wins tonight and drops to 145 pounds, he'll be in line to fight for basically any title in the north-Seattle amateur MMA world. Several of those titles still belong to Chad, so the whole thing would become much less messy if Chad vacated his belts by going professional.

At the door of the gymnasium a boy who looks all of 13 years old is collecting tickets. He looks like he's never seen a press pass before. Poor kid. I walk right by. Growing up is tough.

In the men's room, I'm at a urinal two stalls away from a guy who eats an entire apple—the whole thing—while he urinates. The logistics of how he does this aren't visually confirmed for obvious men's-room courtesy reasons. He washes his hands while holding the core in his mouth, and then throws the core away.

I sit in a section of about two-dozen Jonny fans, including my parents, Brady, Jake, and a guy named Ben, who promises that he's going to provide some "really funny commentary." Ben weighs 275 pounds and has a circumference around his shoulders of 71 inches, which took him "more than one tape measure." At one point in the evening I lose sight of my notebook, and when I get it back someone has added a note next to Ben's name, "Ben, whose shirt is from Baby Gap."

A CageWars staff person is standing on a platform attached to the cage, filming the audience with a handheld camera. His shaky shots of the crowd are displayed on a projector screen that takes up most of the gym's west wall. For about 30 seconds he zooms in on my dad, who has his face in his hands and looks bored. He doesn't notice that he's on the big screen.

Jonny's fight is the 15th of 18 fights tonight. According to someone in our group, we will be here "long enough to watch two movies and still have time to come back and watch Jonny."

FIGHT THREE: 205-POUND MMA

Jake notes that the first fighter "jiggles when he bounces." The fighters end up on the ground, and the jiggler manages to trap both of his opponent's arms and legs while keeping one hand free to pummel his face.

Announcer, "That's what I came to see."

FIGHT FOUR

This fight is what Ben's wife, Ashley, describes as, "This is not a punching one?" This is not a punching one. One of the wrestlers is wearing a red spandex wrestling singlet, with regards to which Ben wants me to write, "Don't do that." The singlet guy gets choked out.

FIGHT FIVE: 170-POUND KICKBOXING

In this fight, large amounts of time are dedicated to recovery from unintentional groin shots. Jake thinks that kicking a guy in the testicles is a good way to take a break if you're tired. Ben yells, "Pee-pee kick! Shake it off!"

When the fight finally resumes, one of the fighters gets punched in the cheek and goes down. In what looks like a Rocky-esque struggle of will, he gets back to his feet before the ref does a ten count. He immediately gets punched even harder in the face, and this time he doesn't get up.

Zipfizz has a banner on the gym wall with their new slogan, "Zipfizz: What's in Your Water?"

FIGHT SEVEN: 115-POUND YOUTH MMA

At one point in this fight a sweaty teenage boy is sitting on another sweaty teenage boy's mouth, punching him in the stomach.

Jonny's dad, "This is getting disgusting."

The face-sitter wins by choking the other kid out. With a chokehold, not by face-sitting. His coach carries him around the ring, Superman-style. His photo is not taken with a ring girl.

FIGHT EIGHT

Jake is asking people for money so that he can buy snacks. This isn't how our family operates, this begging. I tell Jake that if he wants money—a whole dollar—he's going to have to work for it. What he's going to have to do, Brady and I tell him, is he's going to have to go down to the sound table and ask the sound guy if he can wear his hat. The sound guy might be 11 or 12 years old and is wearing an orange knit beanie of the type sometimes used to store large amounts of hair or dreadlocks.

In between rounds, Jake walks down and talks to the sound guy for much longer than seems necessary. The sound guy hands his hat to Jake. Jake puts it on and gives us a sly thumbs up. When Jake gets back we ask him what he was talking to the sound guy about. Jake was making sure the sound guy didn't have lice.

Our next job for Jake—which will earn him $2, for a total of $3, enough to buy a slice of pizza at the concession stand—requires him to go to the Zipfizz booth and ask the Zipfizz girls a series of questions, some involving Zipfizz, some involving whether the Zipfizz girls have boyfriends and, if not, whether they want boyfriends. Our mom overhears parts of this conversation and just gives Jake $2.

FIGHT NINE: 300-POUND KICKBOXING

When the fighters walk out, Ben—without anyone saying anything to provoke him—says, "I don't carry my weight there."

By round three, both fighters look ready to collapse from exhaustion. Not sure how they weren't prepared for this, for a fight going three rounds. Couldn't have taken them by surprise. They both look like they'd rather just sit down for a little while than continue to throw weak and sloppy punches.

FIGHT TEN

This might be the first MMA fight ever to feature a Tiffany fighting a Gabby. Both are white girls with cornrows.

As they're standing in their corners before the fight, Gabby takes a drink of water and spits it on the floor. Her coach mops it up with a towel. Someone behind me is discussing *Million Dollar Baby*.

For the first minute or so of the fight Tiffany demolishes Gabby. A female audience member yells, "Gabby, you go take it! Take it! You got this! You got this thing!"

This just isn't true. Gabby does not have this thing. Tiffany throws a left jab, another left jab, a kick to Gabby's ribs, and then decks Gabby right in the teeth. Gabby crumples so dramatically it looks faked. It's over.

FIGHT ELEVEN

One of the guys spends much of the fight on his back with his feet in the air. This appears to be an impenetrable defense. The other guy is standing, but he just can't get past his opponent's feet. When the guy on his feet tries to run behind, the guy on his back simply spins. It's brilliant.

When they're both on their feet later in the fight, the guy that was on his back gets kneed hard in the hamstring four times. He loses.

Announcer, "I'd like to thank our promoters for getting us in such a beautiful venue with a TV [i.e., the projector screen] like that. Ooh."

FIGHT TWELVE

A man is walking through the bleachers distributing squares of glossy cardstock promoting a musical artist called "Chad Walker Is Big Mouth." The man tells us that Chad Walker is one and the same as our announcer tonight. He says that Chad Walker Is Big Mouth's music contains "no swearing. It's all about recovery."

The paper states that Chad Walker Is Big Mouth's debut album, *Unconscious*—released on the label Puget Sound, Inc.—is available for free download for a limited time. I promise myself that I will download this album at the nearest Internet connection.

Meanwhile, at the actual fight, a guy throws a punch, slips, falls on his back, and the other guy pounces and drops fists on his face. It's over. It all happened so fast. And the only way I can see a replay is to go to JR Phinickey's for the official after party.

The announcer/Chad Walker Is Big Mouth, "Woo!"

FIGHT THIRTEEN

One of Brady's observant and trustworthy friends says to Brady, "How does everyone in your family have such perfect hair? I mean, how thick it is."

In this fight, the fighters tie up and swat at each other a little, but the real damage is done when one fighter repeatedly knees the other one straight in the gut. That's actually what ends the fight. One guy knees the other guy so hard in the stomach that he crumples and doesn't get up for quite some time.

FIGHT FOURTEEN

The first fighter, Josiah, is a sergeant from the U.S. Marine Corps. The second fighter is from Wyoming. We don't really have a choice who to root for in this one. Somehow the guy from Wyoming ends up on his back while the Marine Corps guy stands above him and drops punches onto his face.

FIGHT FIFTEEN: JONNY'S FIGHT

We really don't know much about Jonny's opponent. In general, it seems that whenever we don't know much about a fighter, he isn't exactly a ringer. It takes experience to get good at MMA, so it's rare that someone will be an excellent fighter if no one's ever seen them fight or heard of them. Either way, this is still a fairly important fight for Jonny's career. It's the number-one contender fight, which means that the winner of this fight gets to fight the reigning CageWars 155-pound champion. I'm not sure how there's a reigning CageWars champion, this being the inaugural CageWars event, but I've learned it's best to just keep this sort of question to myself.

In the first round, Jonny gets a takedown and he and his opponent get tangled on the mat for the rest of the round. At one point, Ben barks and it sounds like a real dog. Jonny didn't do much, but he kept his opponent from doing anything at all, so he won the round.

Second round, Jonny's opponent throws a huge punch that misses, Jonny ducks and gets a takedown, and they get tangled for the rest of the round. Jonny has now won two rounds, which means that he wins unless he gets knocked out, or choked out, or irreparably broken in the third round. So it's in Jonny's interest to play it safe and do exactly what he did the first two rounds. He gets a takedown and, yes, they get tangled on the mat. Someone yells, "Keep using that forehead, Jonny, grind it." When the round ends, Jonny has won the fight.

Jonny's fight is what an educated MMA fan would call "smart." Someone who came here tonight looking for some chaos at the college—some no-holds-barred bloodbaths—might call it boring. This is one of the interesting things about how MMA is often marketed. Underneath all the "Ultimates" and "Ax Fighting" and "Cages" and "blood," there's a real sport, a technical sport, and sometimes that sport is more about strategy and cool-headed thinking than blood and violence.

FIGHT EIGHTEEN:
185-POUND CAGEWARS TITLE FIGHT

The announcer encourages us to "support our local economy" by going to JR Phinickey's for the official after party, where we'll get to watch full-length videos of all the fights, the very fights we've been watching for the last three hours.

This fight is between Brent "Mankill" Knopp and Carl Edwards. The last time we saw Mankill was in his fight against Nerd Rage. This one looks more evenly matched. In fact, Carl looks almost identical to Mankill. They're the same height, bald, and muscular in a way that makes me want to go do bench press. The only difference is that Mankill is Caucasian and Carl is African American.

Mankill and Carl look about even in the first round—they punch each other, tackle each other, and dish out enough violence to more than make up for Jonny's fight. In the second round Mankill punches Carl hard with his right hand and follows it with an even harder left. Carl goes down and doesn't get up until we're almost out the door.

Later, at home, I listen to Chad Walker Is Big Mouth's album, *Unconscious*. I've heard much worse hip-hop music. The production is solid, and Chad Walker Is Big Mouth has decent rapping skills. It's his lyrics that are the real standout, though. Contrary to what I was told, there are a few swear words—"*Who fucking farted?*" is a line—and a few lines that don't technically have swearing but are probably R-rated nonetheless, "*I only licky licky if it's that good, I only hit the sticky if it's that good.*" Or, "*Lick my balls and fill up my belly.*"

I never paid Jake his dollar.

CHAPTER 14

WHAT HAPPENED TO FLAT TOP

IN LATE 2010, A muscular young African American man dressed in a gold-and-black rubber-and-spandex outfit appeared in Seattle. He called himself Phoenix Jones, and said he was there to fight crime. He was a superhero, he said. A woman driving a white Kia would drop Phoenix Jones off in the less-safe parts of Seattle, and he'd walk around stopping—or attempting to stop—petty crimes. Phoenix Jones even formed a gang of other superheroes, called The Rain City Superhero Movement. The Rain City Superhero Movement also included Phoenix's wife, who went by the name Purple Reign. Like a true superhero, Phoenix didn't reveal his true identity, although it seems like the proper authorities could've figured it out if they'd given a care.

At a poker game at Brady's house a few months after this started, Jonny told us that he had a story that we just had to hear. He said that a few weeks earlier he'd been looking at the Facebook page for Phoenix Jones, Real-Life Superhero. He was looking at the photos on the fan page, most of which were of Phoenix Jones posing with the good female citizens of Seattle, or of Phoenix Jones in his spandex taking photos of himself in the mirror. In one of the latter type of photos—one that showed Phoenix's pectorals but not his face—Jonny noticed a distinctive tattoo across Phoenix Jones's chest. Jonny had seen this tattoo before.

Jonny sent Phoenix Jones a message. Jonny told Phoenix that it was him, Jonny Gilbertson, from Charlie's Combat Club. He knew that Phoenix Jones was really Ben Fodor, a.k.a. Flat Top, the MMA fighter who had also trained at Charlie's Combat Club. Jonny told him that he'd keep Flat Top's identity a secret, but that if Flat Top didn't want anyone else to know his true identity, he'd better take down that photo. Jonny never heard back from Phoenix Jones. The photo disappeared.

If you're an avid news-consuming citizen, you already know all about Phoenix Jones. He's somewhat of a minor celebrity, appearing in *The Huffington Post*, *Good Morning America*, and pretty much all of Seattle's local news outlets, which seem to get their news from each other. Local opinion on Phoenix Jones ranges from "deeply misguided individual" (the Seattle City Attorney) to "I'm still waiting for Jones to screw up and end up killing someone who is innocent. Maybe then the city will put an end to this screwed up superhero crap for good" (cheery Internet commenter).

To no one's surprise, one night Phoenix Jones tried to break up a drug deal downtown and was stabbed several times. He also got arrested once, for assault charges that involved pepper spray, which is apparently his crime-deterrent of choice. No charges were filed, but Phoenix showed up at court anyway, wearing his mask, and then outside the courthouse gave reporters a speech that would've made Erin Brockovich proud:

"I will continue to patrol with my team, probably tonight. In addition to being Phoenix Jones, I am also Ben Fodor, father and brother. I am just like everybody else. The only difference is that I try to stop crime in my neighborhood and everywhere else. I think I have to look toward the future and see what I can do to help the city."

Phoenix and his team did indeed continue patrolling downtown Seattle, breaking up fights and generally being half-assed vigilantes. At some point in all this, Ben lost his day job teaching life skills to children with autism, reportedly because of his extracurricular activities. When things really got interesting in the Phoenix Jones saga is when a local Seattle supervillain emerged, calling himself Rex Velvet. Through a series of well-made videos released on the Internet, Rex Velvet asked the citizens of Seattle to join him in ridding the city of Phoenix Jones and his silly Rain City Superheroes. The videos were obviously a complete and not even that subtle joke, but Phoenix Jones took the bait. He had a heated debate with Rex Velvet on a local radio station where he called Rex "the Kim Kardashian of villains." Rex Velvet then used the media attention to market a line of Rex Velvet merchandise.

Phoenix Jones still makes appearances on the streets of Seattle, usually at events or protests where media will be present. He has disbanded the Rain City Superheroes, preferring lone-wolf vigilante justice to teamwork vigilante justice. You'll hear news reports of his shenanigans every now and then, reminding you that Phoenix Jones is still a thing that exists in this world.

We're now very far from the world of amateur MMA. But I'm going to posit that Ben Fodor's superhero activities tell us quite a bit about MMA. I can't claim to know exactly why someone would become a vigilante crime-fighting superhero, but it seems reasonable to say that it has something to do with wanting attention, enjoying conflict, and being slightly to entirely crazy. So the way I see it, Ben Fodor first tried to get these things from MMA and then thought, *Nope, I need something that will get me more attention, that will provide more conflict, and that's a good deal crazier,* and the only thing he could think of that beat MMA in all these categories was donning a custom spandex outfit and breaking up drug deals with his bare hands.

CHAPTER 15

CHAD'S LAST AMATEUR FIGHT

HERE WE ARE ONCE again at Edmonds Community College, where earlier in the week a student was stabbed in the face and robbed. Tonight Chad is finally fighting Drew "The Eternal Fire" Brokenshire for the *Ax Fighting* 145-pound mixed martial arts title.

We've been waiting a long time for this fight. This is the first time in almost two years that Chad's had a fight where he wasn't a heavy favorite. In my opinion, Chad's a slight favorite in this fight. Drew has fifteen wins and four losses, while Chad has ten wins and just the one (avenged) loss from his first fight. I'd say those stats favor Chad, but my parents disagree. They tell me they've heard rumors about how Drew trains for MMA full-time and is one of the best fighters in Western Washington. When I investigate further I learn that these rumors originated from Chad.

Chad also has a nagging hand injury, and we're not quite sure how severe it is. It's tough to get a straight story about this sort of thing when there are worried parents involved. He might just have a jammed thumb or a sore muscle, or his hand might be broken. We're not sure—we don't even think that Chad's sure how severe it is—but Chad has decided that it's an injury that can handle a fight.

While I'm waiting in the hallway outside the gym, a man walking by says, "It smells like doo doo in here."

It's true. It does smell like doo doo in here. I soon discover that this is because there is actual doo doo on the hallway's linoleum floor, smeared around in a way that makes it impossible to visually determine what sort of creature the doo doo came from.

Inside the gym Jake greets me with an urgent 13-year-old's story that involves his friend Michael and a limousine and really I have no idea what he's talking about. We walk by an unoccupied wheelchair with a "Yes We Did" Barack Obama sticker.

I'm here with my parents, MBW, and my co-worker Sonjia and her husband, who as I understand it are here for a horizon-expanding cultural experience, sort of like how middle-class families will help at the food bank at Christmas to see how the other half lives.

There are 18 fights tonight, and Chad's is last. My dad, "Let's hope the first seventeen are quick."

FIGHT ONE: 155-POUND MMA

This one's between Joe "The Savage" Val and Elis Armenderaz. Throughout the fight Elis's coaches yell what sounds like a single Spanish word repeated over and over, "Derecha! Derecha! Derecha!"

Joe and Elis get in a belly-to-belly position on the ground where Elis is hugging Joe and Joe is trying to get out of the hug by violently and repeatedly thrusting his hips. Sonjia asks what this is called, and my dad says, "The Saturday Night Special."

After The Savage pounds Elis in the head enough to end the fight, Sonjia notes that she feels really bad just even watching this.

FIGHT TWO

This is the first MMA event I've attended where there's been an African American ring girl.

MBW, "Well, she's kind of black."

For some unknown reason my dad begins telling someone near him that I'm adopted but quickly rescinds his comment. "I was there when you were born," he says. "Believe me. I could tell you about it."

Brady says that it's hard to tell whether the poop in the hallway was dog or human.

FIGHT THREE: 160-POUND KICKBOXING

One of the fighters, Matt, has a tiny torso, disproportionately long arms and legs, and an overall spidery shape. Apparently this is the ideal body shape for a kickboxer. The other guy, Vit, is about as tall as one of Matt's legs. So when Matt kicks, Vit's head is just sitting there like a plump T-ball. Matt kicks Vit in the eyes, knees him in the forehead, and then plants his foot straight into Vit's face. Vit gets knocked down four times and gets back up each time. Which is quite honorable, since Vit hasn't so much as landed a kick all fight. The fifth time Vit goes down, the ref stops the fight.

One of the ring girls tonight is probably most tactfully described in Sonjia's words, "She has more confidence than I do. If I looked like that, I wouldn't be in there."

FIGHT FOUR: 125-POUND MMA

This fight raises the question of how bad it could really hurt to get punched by an adult male who weighs 125 pounds. Apparently, not that bad. These guys trade punches for the whole fight but can't even knock each other down.

MBW's further thoughts on the ring girl who is clearly African American, "She's probably mostly black but probably something else too."

FIGHT FIVE

MBW, "See now, that guy is black."

This African American guy—whose coach is wearing a "Rodman" jersey—punches his opponent so hard it sends his mouthguard several rows deep into the audience.

FIGHT SEVEN: 145-POUND MMA

Steve, "Boring. I'm lucky I had a nap today."

FIGHT NINE: 205-POUND KICKBOXING

This fight confirms what you probably would've guessed: don't fight someone named Bo Reedus. He'll kick your ass. Or at least that's what he'll do for two rounds, until he completely runs out of gas, just like you'd expect from someone named Bo Reedus.

T-SHIRT TEXT SEEN TONIGHT
Fight Me
Talk Shit, Get Hit
The Stronger the Team, the Stronger the Fighter
Watch Your Mouth
Submission Factory
Recycle More Humans

FIGHT TEN: 115-POUND MMA
Right when the fight starts, the fighter in the red corner grabs his opponent around the neck and lifts him off the ground until he can't breathe and has to tap out.

FIGHT TWELVE: 130-POUND WOMEN'S MMA
One of the girls, Tiffany, comes out to a song that features the lyric *"eat, drink, and shut the fuck up."* Tiffany is a truly scary looking young lady. In the first round she gets an arm-bar thing on her opponent—a totally normal-looking girl named Erika—and it seems that Tiffany is intentionally hyper-extending Erika's elbow far enough to cause her pain but not far enough to end the fight. She then somehow crawls on Erika's back and chokes her out until the ref stops the fight. Erika is crying.

My dad, "And a good time was had by all."

FIGHT FIFTEEN: 125-POUND WOMEN'S KICKBOXING
One of the girls here is wearing some sort of a pink skirt. She's tall and pale and, in my mom's words, "looks like a clarinet player." The other fighter is the Regan girl we've seen fight before.

The clarinet-player girl has that same spidery kickboxer shape, which means that for Regan to get close enough to land a few punches she has to take a few kicks to the head. It's a battle of very weak kicks versus very weak punches. These two could fight all night without knocking each other out.

After the fight ends the announcer announces that the judges have reached a split decision, which means that one of the judges disagreed with the other two.

The announcer, "Judge one scores the fight at 29–28 for Griffith. Judge two scores the fight at 29–28 for Benedetti."

After about ten seconds of dramatic silence the announcer says, "Wait, the math is hard here."

There's then an excitement-killing minute of whispering between the announcer and the judges, and finally it's announced that Regan Benedetti won the fight.

FIGHT SIXTEEN: 155-POUND MMA

I'm trying to maintain some sort of journalistic neutrality, but dear Lord this Jeff guy, total asshole, right? There's something about him—maybe the fact that he gelled his hair before the fight—that just deserves a beating. He wins his fight, unfortunately, and yells and jumps up and down, just the way a total asshole would.

FIGHT SEVENTEEN

The program labels this one a *130 MMA Super Fight*, but no explanation is ever given about what the "super" means. The fight itself isn't all that super.

CHAD'S FIGHT

This fight goes far beyond just the *Ax Fighting* 145-pound title belt. This is Chad's big fight, or the biggest fight he's had since his fight with Jonathan Moore. I suspect that, win or lose, this will be Chad's last amateur fight. Drew is the last tough opponent for Chad in the north-Seattle amateur MMA circuit, so even if Chad loses he doesn't have anyone else to fight—he'll still have to go professional. This fight, then, might be the defining fight of his amateur career. Lose, and it'll be remembered that he beat Jonathan Moore and a bunch of slouches but then lost his only really big fight. Win, and he'll have torn his way through the amateur ranks, winning every fight but his first and beating every challenger the area had to offer.

After introducing Chad "Crombie" Douglas and Drew "The Eternal Fire" Brokenshire, the announcer says that they have "the two best records in the state." This is too vague to prove or disprove. This is a five-round fight. Unless someone gets some sort of knockout or TKO, whoever wins the most rounds wins the fight.

In the first round, Drew lands a few weak punches and Chad stomps on his foot. Chad is grabbing Drew's legs and trying to take him down, but Drew is up against the ropes and isn't budging. It's clear from my family's reaction that they're not used to watching Chad fight people he can't take down at will. At the very end of the round they hit the mat, but it's obvious that Drew won the round.

In the second round, Chad gets his takedown, but Drew rolls around and ends up on Chad's back, punching him in the head and then getting a tight chokehold around Chad's neck. Drew holds the choke for about 30 seconds. Somehow Chad escapes and punches Drew a few times before the round ends. It seems like Drew won this round, but I really don't know how they score chokeholds.

At the start of round three, Chad does a spinning backhand punch that hits Drew without much force. For most of the round they roll around and grab at each other's limbs. I'm not sure what's going on, much less who's scoring points. At one point Drew gets on Chad's back and gets a firm chokehold on Chad. It looks like Chad can't breathe for about 30 seconds, but then the round ends.

By my uneducated count, Drew has won all three rounds so far. This judgment is based only on my perception and not on any sort of real scoring system. My parents seem to think Chad won round three, but that might be their parental supportiveness speaking.

If Drew indeed won the first three rounds, then Chad can win only by knocking Drew out or getting some form of technical knockout—that is, getting Drew to tap out or getting things to a point where the ref stops the fight.

They start the fourth round on their feet throwing punches, and then amidst the punches Chad gets another takedown. He's been able to do this several times so far, but this is the first time that he's been able to do anything with it. He starts hammering Drew's face with his forearms. Chad then switches to choking Drew for a while, and then, when Drew rolls out of the choke, Chad gets back on top of him and delivers a solid beating. Chad finishes the round with Drew bent in half and choked. My dad says, "The pike position."

Chad definitely won that round. Everyone around me seems to think that Chad and Drew have each won two rounds, which means that the winner of this final round wins the fight. I'm not so sure, but there's really not time to discuss it.

Announcer, "Who is the toughest 145-pounder?"

Chad starts the final round by driving Drew into the ropes. Drew lands several solid knees as Chad gets another takedown. My dad almost falls off the bleachers. Chad lands some punches and then gets his arms around Drew's neck. Drew gets out and wraps his legs around Chad's head. I have no idea whether this is an actual move. The referee is blocking most of the action, but it appears that Drew is punching Chad's head.

The round ends. The fight is over. My family is celebrating as though Chad has won. Both Chad and Drew are celebrating as though they've won.

Announcer, "Let's make sure we get this one right."

Someone from the judges' table hands the announcer a slip of paper, and then he announces that, by unanimous decision, our winner and new *Ax Fighting* 145-pound champion is Chad Douglas. There's no way around it now. This is the end of Chad's amateur fighting career. If he ever fights again, it will be professional. But as it'll turn out, this fight, at any level, amateur or professional, is Chad's last fight.

EPILOGUE

ONE OF THE FRUSTRATING parts about following an amateur sport is that you're not guaranteed a climactic seven-game playoff or a trophy ceremony at an all-you-can-eat pizza place. Since amateur MMA doesn't have a distinct season or even a rhythm to its competitions, you don't get any of the satisfaction of knowing what comes next.

With Chad's career, we never knew at the time whether a fight was the apex of his career or just a prerequisite for more important fights. We did know that his fights with Jonathan Moore and Drew Brokenshire were more important than, say, his tag-team match, but we didn't know how important they'd be in the scale of his overall career. If Chad started fighting professionally, then those early amateur fights would still be just that, amateur.

In retrospect, it looks like Chad's fight with Drew was the best climax we're going to get. Chad went into that fight with what he later learned was a broken hand and, as one would expect, a five-round MMA fight didn't help the healing process. In the last three months, he hasn't been able to punch things, and it doesn't appear that he'll be able to punch things anytime in the foreseeable future. You can't fight if you can't punch things. And you especially can't fight in a professional fight if you can't punch things.

But even now, we don't get the closure of knowing that Chad is for sure done fighting. He says that in a few months he's going to go into the gym and punch something. If his hand survives, he might continue fighting. My opinion—and it's just an opinion—is that for the story of Chad's amateur-fighting career, his fight with The Eternal Fire was the best ending we're going to get.

So, what we have tonight is an epilogue. The two other fighters I've been following—Billy Walker and Jonny Gilbertson—are both fighting for title belts at an event called *Chaos at the College 2*. Tonight we also get to watch the debut fight from Ben McKinley, a color commentator from a previous fight who claims he has a chest circumference of 72 inches. Ben claims that this will be his only MMA fight, a once-in-a-lifetime event that happens to take place on his wife's birthday. His wife's attitude about this coincidence is best described as "tolerant."

I don't even have to show my press pass to get into the fights. I just walk in with a group of people. I sit with my dad, my mom, Brady, and Jake. Jake has somehow acquired a bag filled with what looks like a pound of Mike & Ike's and Runts. Jake tries telling me that banana Runts are his favorite. My dad is having a conversation about an anal catheter and how he thinks it's a good idea.

PRE-FIGHT INTERVIEW WITH BEN

Q: "Ben, what's your strategy going into tonight's fight?"
A: "Win."

FIGHT ONE

The announcer, after saying that "the action is going to be intense tonight," tells us that the first fight is cancelled because one of the fighters didn't show. The fighter who did show gets to stand in the cage and wave to the crowd.

Our announcer is Chad Walker, also known as the musical artist Chad Walker Is Big Mouth. When Chad Walker Is Big Mouth talks, he makes the same hand motions that hip-hop artists do in music videos. The hand motions seem subconscious and involuntary. Out of all the MMA announcers we've seen, Chad Walker Is Big Mouth is by far the most talented.

FIGHT TWO

Jake bets a dollar on Andy Baker, who isn't even in this fight. Andy Baker was the fighter whose opponent didn't show up for the first fight. Jake agrees that he owes me a dollar just for being dumb.

In the actual fight, one of the fighters lifts his opponent, turns him upside down, and drops him on his head.

Guy behind me, "That shit is all fucked up."

FIGHT THREE

The first fighter—whom the announcer calls "Chops"—comes out to a song that begins "*Let the bodies hit the floor. Let the bodies hit the floor.*" Doesn't seem totally appropriate for an MMA fight, where there's really only one body he's supposed to let hit the floor.

When the other fighter walks out, my dad says, "It looks a little unfair here. You got the kid with the farmer tan."

The kid with the farmer's tan ends up on his back and gets punched in the face nine times. The ref lets the fight continue, and the first round ends. In the second round, the kid with the farmer's tan comes out swinging and misses twice. On his third try he lands a jab on Chops's nose. Chops crumples. The kid with the farmer's tan wins. The crowd goes nuts.

FIGHT FOUR

One of the fighters is bleeding. I don't know which one, and I can't see where the wound is, but the fighters are now wrestling in a patch of blood that's about six square feet and growing.

Someone finally gets punched enough for the ref to end the fight. We're left with a patch of blood that covers about 20 percent of the ring, not including bloody footprints around the perimeter. Someone tosses the ref a white towel. He gets on his knees and starts scrubbing.

The ref pauses from scrubbing and appears to wipe the sweat off his brow with the same towel he's been using to scrub the blood. The net effect of the scrubbing is that the bloodstain has expanded to now cover about 25 percent of the ring. Brady says that if he ever murders someone, this is the guy he's calling to clean it up. The ref stands, looks down at the blood, and appears to shrug. The next fighters are called to the ring.

FIGHT FIVE

Jake is bored—this is a women's 125-pound kickboxing match—and wants to know if there are any tasks that I would pay him money to do. I offer Jake $5 if he can convince the preadolescent-looking DJ to play "Wake Me Up Before You Go-Go" by Wham! Jake is not aware of this song but accepts the explanation that it's the song you're least likely to hear at an amateur MMA event.

Jake talks to the announcer and convinces him to write down the song's name. Jake later sends one of his friends to request the same song. This friend returns and tells us that the DJ said, "We don't take requests, yo."

Jake, like Jonny, started wrestling when he was around four. Jake is already an elite wrestler. He's won two kids' state championships, and he has the potential to win a few high school state championships, according to our mom. I keep telling our mom that, if Jake keeps it up with the wrestling, it's almost inevitable that he'll someday end up doing MMA. Some of Jake's little wrestling friends have already started going to Charlie's Combat Club. Our mom has strictly forbidden Jake from setting foot in Charlie's, but really with Jake's wrestling prowess and exposure to MMA it can only be a matter of time before we get to watch the MMA debut of Jake "Cookie" Douglas.

FIGHT SIX

A few CageWars staff guys finally bring out a mop and liquid to clean up the blood. Announcer, "Cleanup on aisle three."

This fight is between an African American and a Caucasian. The person sitting next to me says something so racially insensitive that I refuse to write it down.

In round one, the African American fighter gets on the Caucasian fighter's back and chokes him out. To celebrate his victory, the winning fighter lies in the center of the cage and does three snow angels.

The person sitting next to me, "No, I meant the white guy. The white guy looks like a gorilla."

FIGHT SEVEN: BEN'S HEAVYWEIGHT FIGHT

Ben told us—and promised his wife—that this will be his only fight. Participating in an MMA fight is apparently something Ben wants to check off his bucket list, like how some people want to skydive or see Italy in the fall.

Ben has at least a 17-inch advantage in chest circumference over his opponent, which means that his opponent has a six-inch advantage in height. Early in the first round, Ben's opponent tries to kick him. Ben catches his leg and then kicks the guy's other leg, knocking him down with the sort of thud you only hear in heavyweight fights. Ben jumps onto the guy's back but somehow slips off and ends up on his own back, with the other guy on top—not only on top, but sitting on Ben's chest and trapping both Ben's arms, punching him in the face until the ref ends the fight.

I'm later told that Ben now plans on fighting again.

FIGHT EIGHT

One of the fighters here, Jaimin, comes out with a posse of guys wearing shirts that say "Hawaii Boyz." One of them is waving a red, green, and yellow flag that I'm assuming is the Hawaiian flag. The announcer tells us that we have a few guys here who've come all the way from Hawaii to fight tonight.

The guy from Team Hawaii Boyz gets beat in about 45 seconds.

FIGHT NINE

This fight features the second and final fighter from Team Hawaii Boyz. There's the same ruckus with all the "Hawaii Boyz" shirts and the flag.

Right after the fight starts, before the fighters have even touched each other, the Hawaii Boy, while just standing there, grabs his shoulder and falls. He doesn't get up. His coaches enter the ring and tend to him.

Sources report that the Hawaii Boy swung his shoulder and threw it out. Same sources wonder where his Hawaiian flag is now.

The Hawaii Boy eventually gets up. The announcer says that the Hawaii Boy is unable to continue the fight due to injury. The other fighter gets his arm raised and gets a trophy.

A middle-aged man sitting near me says, "He's just a pussy. That's all there is to it. Never seen anything like it."

FIGHT ELEVEN

When I first started watching MMA, most fights seemed riveting or at least worth watching, for the novelty if nothing else. But now, watching fights like this one, fights between two below-average fighters I don't know, I start thinking about all the Saturday evenings I've spent watching sweaty young adults trying to grab each other's legs—or, worse, playing paddle fisties on the mat—and how boring it can be. Even the guy climbing the cage and straddling and then sort of humping the cross-post after he wins—even though "that's what [the announcer] came to see"—it's just not that exciting anymore.

ADDITIONAL EPILOGATORY MATERIAL

As a fan, the most frustrating part about how Chad's career ended is that I never found out exactly how good he was, that I never got to see him take that beating. Chad's fight with Drew was close enough that I'm tempted to say that Chad was just slightly better than Drew, but that might be misleading—some athletes perform to the level of their competition, and Chad might've been that sort of athlete. If I had to guess, I'd say that Chad probably would've had a winning record as a low-level pro—five wins and three losses sounds about right—but that he wouldn't be able to advance past that level before age and injuries caught up with him. But I really have no idea.

As a fan, this is frustrating. But it also strikes me as shrewd. Chad gets to end his MMA career with a flawless record—his one loss avenged—and the question of how good he really was is left to people's imaginations. It's like the old bit about horror stories: when the monster's revealed, it's always less terrifying than when the monster was behind the door and existed only in your imagination. Chad ended his MMA career with the monster behind the door, and no one knows how tough he really is.

Even though Chad seems to be done fighting, I doubt he'll leave MMA behind entirely. He enjoys coaching and working out, he's made some of his best friends through MMA, and the void it leaves in his life won't be easy to fill. He'll get to keep all his trophies, but I'm not sure about all the belts. He may have to give those back. I still don't really know how the whole belt system works. Although MMA will be tough to out-extreme, Chad will likely move on to a new extreme venture. As of this writing, Chad is turning in his application to be an astronaut, and on a recent trip to Vegas with Charlie and Billy he got a Charlie's Combat Club tattoo on his arm.

It's hard for me to gauge what sort of effect MMA has had on Chad's life, so I asked our mom. Her maternal opinion is that it's been a mild positive. That, yes, it's never really a great thing when you permanently damage your punching/writing hand, but other than that she can't really think of any real negative effect from all that MMA. It's not like he's throwing off everything else in his life to make room for MMA—during his MMA career, he's had several promotions at work, logged more than 30 days of snowboarding per year, and basically been a professor emeritus in the local wakeboarding scene. And, as far as his personal social life, he's definitely made more friends and had a better community through MMA than he has at, say, Boeing. MMA has certainly eaten up a lot of Chad's time, time that theoretically could've been spent in more constructive ways, but I strongly suspect that if Chad gave up MMA, he wouldn't spend all that time mentoring at-risk youth or fighting crime or working with Habitat for Humanity.

But still, no good mother steers her children toward MMA.

My opinion—which is based on conversations with Chad and sheer conjecture—is that MMA has been a net positive in Chad's life. If you're wired for MMA—and Chad is indeed wired for MMA—then there's nothing else that can fill the MMA-shaped hole in your life. If Chad hadn't done MMA, he would've always wished he had, and that's a decent reason to do something. And because he did MMA, he got to have experiences that very few of us will ever have: fighting another man in a cage, beating another man in a cage fight, training for high-level athletic competition, getting punched in the face more than any person should, and standing in a ring surrounded by thousands of cheering people. Those are cool things, and Chad likely appreciates them as much as anyone could.

These are powerful experiences, and I strongly suspect that MMA is one of those things that once you do it, you will always miss it. And—according to my theory about why former wrestlers take up MMA—if MMA was shielding Chad from some painful realities about the world, then the adjustment to life as a non-MMA fighter might be difficult. And I'm not sure what sort of long-term effect all of this has on a person.

And so, after more than two years of watching MMA and talking to fighters and pretending to be a journalist, I think I have an answer to why exactly someone would want to fight another person in a cage: MMA is fun—a very specific kind of fun, a kind of fun that doesn't seem like fun to those of us who aren't wired for it, a fun that might be sheltering fighters from realizing what an insignificant loser they are in the big scheme of things, but nonetheless the only real word for it is *fun*. A sort of fun that you just can't get anywhere else.

POST-FIGHT INTERVIEW WITH BEN
"Don't write anything too terrible about me."

FIGHT THIRTEEN

Judging by the sound of the crowd, I'm missing a good fight while waiting in the bathroom line. On the upside, I witness an obese teenager walking out of a bathroom stall with a giant smile.

INTERVIEW WITH A ZIPFIZZ GIRL

I told myself that I was finally going to interview a ring girl tonight. But now that I'm here, all the questions I want to ask seem like they'd come across as sleazy ("Do you change into your swimsuit once you get here, or do you drive here in your swimsuit?"), condescending ("Did you always want to be a ring girl?"), or just pointless ("What's your favorite part about being a ring girl?").

So instead, I opt to interview a Zipfizz girl. A person could at least have a non-sleazy reason to go to the Zipfizz booth and talk to one of the Zipfizz girls, i.e., the purchasing of Zipfizz. The two Zipfizz girls are at the Zipfizz booth near the entrance, trying to peddle their just-add-water energy drink. I approach the table and, in an effort to be nonchalant, read their Zipfizz promotional materials:

"Did you know? Zipfizz is the healthy alternative to energy and sports drinks. It is now available in Walmart. 0 SUGAR. 10 CALORIES. LOW CARB. 41,667% VITAMIN B-12. LOADED WITH ANTIOXIDANTS. 4–6 HOURS OF ENERGY with no crash. Zipfizz is a propriety [sic] blend. Zipfizz advises using 16–20 ounces of water. Drink a sip to make room. Add powder. Shake it up & ENJOY!"

The Zipfizz girls ask if they can help me with anything. One of the Zipfizz girls is substantially better looking than the other. I try to direct my question to the less-good-looking girl, who's probably sick of everyone always interviewing her cuter coworker.

Q: "Yes, actually, I was wondering how one becomes a Zipfizz girl, I mean how did you get this job?"

A: "Uh, my sister's roommate was friends with the marketing director or something and she asked if I wanted to do it."

I consider presenting my press pass and notepad to lend this interview some legitimacy, but I realize that then I might appear to be the sort of person who makes his own fake press pass and brings a creepy notebook to amateur sporting events just so he can have invasive conversations with girls who can't possibly be older than 20.

Q: "And do you enjoy being Zipfizz girls?"

A: "Yeah, we enjoy doing it. It's fun."

This last question was where I really screwed the journalistic pooch. It was a yes-or-no question that couldn't possibly have received an interesting answer. And, worse, after that question all three of us are thinking about the sad facts of the situation: this is a god-awful and—when you think about it—incredibly depressing attempt to hit on a Zipfizz girl. An attempt by someone who doesn't even have it in him to hit on the moderately cute Zipfizz girl. There's only one possible follow-up question:

Q: "How much for a canister of Zipfizz?"

A: "Two dollars each, or three for five dollars."

FIGHT FIFTEEN

Chad Walker Is Big Mouth tells us that the Hawaii Boyz would like to say something. One of them is handed the microphone. He can't seem to achieve the proper face-to-microphone distance, so I only catch one sentence, "Thank you for not booing us."

One of the fighters here, Colton, has a cheering section that contains no fewer than nine screaming adolescent girls. One of Colton's coaches is wearing a T-shirt that says, "HANDS UP, CHIN DOWN, NUTS HANG, FISTS SWING." Colton wins by split decision.

FIGHT SEVENTEEN: BILLY'S FIGHT

Billy Walker is fighting Jose "The Rasta" Garza. Billy has nine wins and four losses and has no known relation to Chad Walker. The Rasta has nine wins and two losses, one of which was to a guy now fighting in the UFC. The Rasta appears to be Mexican and has nothing visibly Rastafarian about his appearance.

In the first round, The Rasta reveals a tactic I haven't seen before. While they're on their feet, as soon as Billy steps in for a takedown, The Rasta grabs Billy and falls on his back, pulling Billy on top of him. I'm not sure who gets points for this setup, which makes it impossible for me to know who won the first two rounds.

In the third round, Billy lands a punch that knocks The Rasta to his butt. Billy jumps on him, but the Rasta grabs Billy's arm and scissors it with his legs. Maybe this is what he's been trying to do from his back this whole time. The Rasta scissors Billy's arm for a few tense seconds, and then Billy slips out.

In round four, the announcer says, "This is where the training in the gym pays off." The Rasta must have trained by grabbing people and then falling on his back, because this is what he continues to do—although I still don't see what he's hoping to accomplish. Round five is the same story. Unless you get a bonus for falling to your back with your opponent on top of you, then Billy won. The judges confirm it. Billy wins the CageWars 135-pound MMA title by unanimous decision.

FIGHT EIGHTEEN: JONNY'S FIGHT

Jonny, who's more or less replacing Chad as one of the premier 145-pound fighters in the north-Seattle amateur mixed martial arts circuit, is fighting Drew Brokenshire—the same Drew Brokenshire that Chad defeated in his last fight. It's a nice changing-of-the-guard moment. The consensus among Jonny fans is that this is a tough fight for Jonny. Jonny's a better athlete and a much better wrestler than Drew, but Drew has a substantial advantage in experience.

My Zipfizz friends enter the ring to distribute Zipfizz. As a special treat, the ring girls join them, like it's a girls-of-amateur-MMA finale.

At the start of the first round, Jonny lands a few kicks and then shoots for Drew's legs. As Jonny's doing this, Drew punches him in the head. Jonny ends up on top of Drew on the ground, but they soon get back to their feet. At the end of the round, Jonny does this flick-throw thing to get Drew off him that doesn't accomplish much but looks cool. Not sure who won that round.

The second round starts with a section of the crowd chanting, "Jonny! Jonny! Jonny!" and ends with Jonny on his back trying to kick Drew. In between, Drew landed a few kicks and Jonny got a takedown. Drew probably won that round.

At the start of round three, Jonny takes Drew down with a bear hug, but then Jonny ends up on his hands and knees with Drew on his back punching the sides of Jonny's face. If I've learned anything about MMA, it's that you don't want someone on your back punching you in the face. Drew stops punching Jonny and wraps his arm around Jonny's neck. After about 15 seconds, Jonny taps out. Drew wins. Jonny is now four and one and has plenty of fights ahead of him, and we'll all get to watch MMA for years to come, if that's how we want to spend our Saturday evenings.

Chad Walker Is Big Mouth must have sensed that it's a special moment, the end of an MMA story. As people leave he says, "Folks, you don't have to go home, but you can't stay here."

ACKNOWLEDGMENTS

I WOULD LIKE TO acknowledge the following people for making this book possible.

My family—Laura Belle, my mom, my dad, Chad, Brady, and Jake—for supporting this project and being endlessly quotable.

Chad (again), Billy, Jonny, Charlie, and the rest of the fighters for beating people up/getting beat up for my journalistic benefit and generally being more tolerant and open to being written about than I had any right to expect.

John Warner at McSweeney's for giving this concept a chance in the first place and for encouraging it along the way. And all the rest of the folks at McSweeney's—Chris Monks, Jordan Bass—for continuing to provide a place for great and funny writing. This seems like a good place to acknowledge that much of this material originally appeared on McSweeney's in a different form.

Eve Connell, Greg Gerding, and the rest of the folks at University of Hell Press.

Ryan Boudinot, Kay Harkins, Micheline Aharonian Marcom, Karl Martin, Dean Nelson, and Carl Winderl for their encouragement and guidance on how to write things people might actually want to read.

Everyone else quoted or described in these pages—Franklin, Bruce, Ben, et al—for doing/saying something noteworthy. I should also acknowledge (although it's probably obvious) that some names have been changed.

ABOUT THE AUTHOR

Rory Douglas lives in Washington with his wife, dog, and son. His writing has appeared in *McSweeney's*, *The Rumpus*, and *Monkeybicycle*, among other publications.

THIS BOOK IS ONE OF THE MANY AVAILABLE FROM
UNIVERSITY OF HELL PRESS.
DO YOU HAVE THEM ALL?

by **Tyler Atwood**
an electric sheep jumps to greener pasture

by **John W Barrios**
Here Comes the New Joy

by **Eirean Bradley**
the I in team
the little BIG book of Go Kill Yourself

by **Calvero**
someday i'm going to marry Katy Perry
i want love so great it makes Nicholas Sparks cream in his pants

by **Leah Noble Davidson**
Poetic Scientifica
Door

by **Brian S. Ellis**
American Dust Revisited
Often Go Awry

by **Greg Gerding**
The Burning Album of Lame
Venue Voyeurisms: Bars of San Diego
Loser Makes Good: Selected Poems 1994
Piss Artist: Selected Poems 1995–1999
The Idiot Parade: Selected Poems 2000–2005

by **Lauren Gilmore**
Outdancing the Universe

by **Robert Duncan Gray**
Immaculate/The Rhododendron and Camellia Year Book (1966)

by **Joseph Edwin Haeger**
Learn to Swim

by **Lindsey Kugler**
HERE.

by **Wryly T. McCutchen**
My Ugly and Other Love Snarls

by **Johnny No Bueno**
We Were Warriors

by **A.M. O'Malley**
What to Expect When You're Expecting Something Else

by **Stephen M. Park**
High & Dry
The Grass is Greener

by **Christine Rice**
Swarm Theory

by **Michael N. Thompson**
A Murder of Crows

by **Sarah Xerta**
Nothing to Do with Me

UNIVERSITY OF HELL PRESS

*Denting the world with words,
one incendiary book at a time.*

CPSIA information can be obtained at www.ICGtesting.com
Printed in the USA
LVOW11s1007131115

462432LV00004B/50/P

9 781938 753176